1203000 F942

QUE ..., C. H. B.

CW01636440

Please ... date shown.

So tha ... t local rate,
please call the numbers ... w:

	From Area codes 01923 or 0208:	From the rest of Herts:
Renewals:	01923 471373	01438 737373
Enquiries:	01923 471333	01438 737333
Minicom:	01923 471599	01438 737599

L32b

Hertfordshire
COUNTY COUNCIL
Community Information

25 JUL 2001

04 FEB 2003

RECEIVED THE SUM OF

HERTFORDSHIRE LIBRARY SERVICE

24 OCT 2001

WITHDRAWN FOR SALE

SL

4 APR 1985

05 JAN 1990

06 JAN 1993

A HISTORY OF EVERYDAY THINGS IN ENGLAND

Books by the Quennells

A HISTORY OF EVERYDAY THINGS IN ENGLAND

Vol. I. 1066–1499
Vol. II. 1500–1799
Vol. III. 1733–1851
Vol. IV. 1851–1914

EVERYDAY LIFE IN PREHISTORIC TIMES
EVERYDAY LIFE IN ROMAN AND ANGLO-SAXON TIMES
EVERYDAY THINGS IN ANCIENT GREECE

1 Elizabeth Hunting

A HISTORY OF EVERYDAY THINGS IN ENGLAND

II

1500 to 1799

By

MARJORIE & C. H. B. QUENNELL

B. T. BATSFORD LTD
London

First published 1919
Fifth edition 1968
Reprinted 1975, 1979

Revised Edition © Peter Quennell, 1960

To
P. C. Q.
G. E. Q.
&
R. P. Q.

HERTFORDSHIRE
COUNTY LIBRARY
J942
1203000

PRINTED IN GREAT BRITAIN BY THE ANCHOR PRESS LTD
TIPTREE, ESSEX
FOR THE PUBLISHERS
B. T. BATSFORD LTD, 4 FITZHARDINGE STREET, LONDON W1H 0AH
ISBN 0 7134 1651 3

PREFACE

OUR work has been done for boys and girls of any age, and we hope it will be useful in providing a background for school history lessons, and make the historical figures more real by housing and clothing them, showing the games they played and the things they fashioned. But from our own standpoint we shall have failed unless we can as well interest our readers in the way things were made, and encourage them to make and do things themselves.

But leaving craftsmanship till later on, we think a great mistake is made in not seeking to interest boys and girls in architecture, costume, and the arts generally. One can so well argue back from the details of church, house, and dress, to the characteristics of the people who have produced them.

All history embodies a recognition of great movements, which express the hopes and aspirations of a people. The sturdiness of Norman architecture is as typical as the grace and beauty of the thirteenth-century work. The fourteenth and fifteenth centuries showed little organic structural development, and seemed to have few impulses. Decoration was overlaid on older forms. In this Volume II of our book we have tried to show how all the old building, with its furniture, the dresses of the people, and their games, were not playthings, or the sport of fashion as now, but history in stone, wood, and fabrics.

We have tried to present work as a joyous sort of business, and we are quite sure that in the old days the craftsman enjoyed his job, or he would not have taken so much trouble to make quite ordinary things beautiful. If for the last hundred years the reverse has come to be the case, from the historical point of view such a period is only a spasm in the old world's pain; the future belongs to the boys and girls of today, and they must alter things, improve them, and think of other things than money.

We should also like to have drawn a parallel between football and architecture, and shown how the best results are obtained by team-work, rather than by the individual star performer. We want to interest our readers in everyday things, because never was there a period in the world's history when these were of greater importance. We are constantly coming up against such phrases nowadays as "Increasing Production" and "Rate of Exchange".

We all know that the two Great Wars meant the sacrifice of many of the best and noblest lives in the country; that we are all richer by this in one way, and much poorer in another needs little emphasis. We have also wasted enormous quantities of the materials we need for living. Our iron, coal, wood, and all kinds of other things, have been wrought into shells, and exploded; built into ships, and sent to the bottom of the sea by enemy submarines. So when the statesmen talk of the necessity for increasing production, they mean of all the materials, and everyday things, we need for our life and trade; not that we need more Treasury notes, or money.

If the thing is more important than money, then it is obvious that while we are increasing production, it will be as well to maintain our reputation for making good things. We can only do this if the makers are happy and contented, and think they are fairly treated.

Now as to what is meant by the "Rate of Exchange". Boys and girls often hear that foreign countries will allow us sometimes more, and sometimes less, for the British pound, and there is some excuse for thinking that it is a rate of exchange of money; but this is not the case—in reality it is our old friend, the everyday thing, that is being exchanged. Let us see how this works. Great Britain is a small place, with a large population, and we cannot produce all our food, or the raw materials we need for our industry; but we possess coal, iron, and clever workmen. We go to South America, and in effect say to the people there, "We will exchange ploughs and locomotives for your corn and cattle"; and this they are glad to do, because they cannot make machinery, and they grow more foodstuffs than they can consume. During the wars we could not produce the things which other countries wanted, and offered them money instead, but this was of little use, unless with it, from some other country, they could obtain the desired everyday thing. As these became scarcer all over the world, money had less purchasing power.

2 Costume of the Sixteenth Century

PREFACE

The statesmen, then, want to increase production, so that not only may we be able to supply our own needs, but have something over to exchange for raw materials and food. So the everyday thing is more important than money, and triumphs over it, and, such being the case, quite deserves a little history of its own. But our space is limited, our subject large, and our own knowledge small, so we cannot do more than present an outline sketch, and if we can but stimulate our readers' interest, they themselves must fill in those wide open spaces which we have only skirted.

MARJORIE and C. H. B. QUENNELL

Berkhamsted, Herts

CONTENTS

THE ILLUSTRATIONS

The numerals in parentheses in the text refer to the *figure numbers* of the illustrations

THE ILLUSTRATIONS

THE ILLUSTRATIONS

BIBLIOGRAPHY

Agriculture and the Countryside

Crowther, J. G., *The Story of Agriculture* (Hamilton, 1958).
Fussell, G. E., *The Farmer's Tools, 1500–1900* (Melrose, 1952).
Fussell, G. E., *Village Life in the 18th Century* (Littlebury, 1948).
Fussell, G. E. and K. R., *The English Countryman: His Life and Work, A.D. 1500–1900* (Melrose, 1953).
Trow-Smith, R., *English Husbandry, from the Earliest Times to the Present Day* (Faber, 1951).

Architecture and Houses

Barfoot, A., *Homes in Britain* (Batsford, 1963).
Dutton, R., *The Age of Wren* (Batsford, 1951).
Francis, R., *Looking for Elizabethan England* (Macdonald, 1954).
Francis, R., *Looking for Georgian England* (Macdonald, 1952).
Geffrye Museum, *17th-Century English Homes* (L.C.C., 1958).
Geffrye Museum, *18th-Century English Homes* (L.C.C., 1959).
Godfrey, W. H., *The Story of Architecture in England.* Vol. 2: From Tudor Times to the end of the Georgian period (Batsford, 1931).
Lees-Milne, J., *Tudor Renaissance* (Batsford, 1951).
Lloyd, N., *History of the English House to the Victorian period* (Architectural Press, 1949).
Nye, T., *Parish Church Architecture* (Batsford, 1965).
Summerson, Sir J., *Architecture in Britain, 1530–1830* (Penguin, 1953).
Turnor, R., *The Smaller English House, 1500–1939* (Batsford, 1952).
Yarwood, D., *The Architecture of England* (Batsford, 1963).

Customs and Folk-lore

Bett, H., *English Legends* (Batsford, 1952).
Bett, H., *English Myths and Traditions* (Batsford, 1952).
Hole, C., *English Custom and Usage* (Batsford, 1950).
Turner, E. S., *A History of Courting* (Joseph, 1954).

Decoration and Furniture

Brooke, Iris, *Four Walls Adorned: Interior Decoration 1485–1820* (Methuen, 1952).
Davis, F., *A Picture History of Furniture* (Hulton, 1958).
Dutton, R., *The English Interior, 1500–1900* (Batsford, 1948).
Fastnedge, R., *English Furniture Styles from 1500 to 1830* (Penguin, 1955).
Hayward, C. H., *English Period Furniture:* An account of the evolution of furniture from 1500 to 1850. New ed. (Evans, 1957).
Jourdain, M., *English Interior Decoration, 1500–1830* (Batsford, 1950).
Jourdain, M., and Rose, F., *English Furniture: the Georgian period (1750–1830)* (Batsford, 1953).
Victoria and Albert Museum, *Georgian Furniture*. 2nd ed. (H.M.S.O., 1958).
Yarwood, D., *The English Home* (Batsford, 1956).

Dress and Costume

Bradfield, N. M., *Historical Costumes of England from the Eleventh to the Twentieth Century* (Harrap, 1958).
Brooke, Iris, *Dress and Undress: the Restoration and Eighteenth Century* (Methuen, 1958).
Cunnington, C. W. and P., *Handbook of English Costume in the 16th Century* (Faber, 1954).
Cunnington, C. W. and P., *Handbook of English Costume in the 17th Century* (Faber, 1955).
Cunnington, C. W. and P., *Handbook of English Costume in the 18th Century* (Faber, 1957).
Kelly, F. M., and Schwabe, R., *A Short History of Costume and Armour, chiefly in England, 1066–1800*. Vol. 2, 1485–1800 (Batsford, 1931).
Norris, H., *Costume and Fashion*. Vol. 3. The Tudors, 1495–1603 (Dent, 1938).
Reynolds, G., *Costume of the Western World: Elizabethan and Jacobean, 1558–1625* (Harrap, 1951).

BIBLIOGRAPHY

Rojinskii, L., *17th Century Costume* (Pitman, 1952).
Victoria and Albert Museum, *Costume Illustration: the Seventeenth and Eighteenth Centuries* (H.M.S.O., 1951).
Yarwood, D., *English Costume from the Second Century B.C. to 1960* (Batsford, 1961).

Leisure and Pastimes
Clinton-Baddeley, V. C., *All Right on the Night* (Putnam, 1954).
Craik, T. W., *The Tudor Interlude: Stage, Costume and Acting* (Leicester U.P., 1958).
Hole, C., *English Sports and Pastimes* (Batsford, 1949).
Nicoll, A., *The Development of the Theatre:* a Study of Theatrical Art from the Beginnings to the Present Day. 4th ed. (Harrap, 1958).

Social Life
Allen, A., *Life in Britain since 1700* (Johnston, 1956).
Ashley, M., *England in the 17th Century*. 2nd ed. (Penguin, 1958).
Bagley. J. J., *Life in Medieval England* (Batsford, 1960).
Byrne, M. St. Clare, *Elizabethan Life in Town and Country*. 7th ed. (Methuen, 1954).
Dodd, A. H., *Life in Elizabethan England* (Batsford, 1961).
Finnemore, J., *Social Life in England.* Book 2. From the Fifteenth Century to the end of the Eighteenth Century (Black, 1956).
George, M. D., *England in Transition:* Life and Work in the Eighteenth Century (Penguin, 1953).
Harrison, M., and Bryant, M. E., *Picture Source Book for Social History; 16th Century* (Allen and Unwin, 1951).
Harrison, M., and Wells, A. A. M., *Picture Source Book for Social History; 17th Century* (Allen and Unwin, 1953).
Harrison, M., and Wells, A. A. M., *Picture Source Book for Social History; 18th Century* (Allen and Unwin, 1955).
Hartley, D., and Elliott, M., *Life and Work of the People of England.* Vol. 2. The Renaissance, A.D. 1500–1800 (Batsford, 1931).
Hole, C., *English Home Life, 1500–1800* (Batsford, 1949).
Marshall, D., *English People in the 18th Century* (Longmans, 1956).
Moss, P., *Meals Through the Ages* (Harrap, 1958).
Pearson, L. E., *Elizabethans at Home* (O.U.P., 1957).
Shakespeare's England; An Account of the Life and Manners of his Age. 2 Vols. (O.U.P., 1916).
Trail, H. D., and Mann, J. S., *Social England;* A Record of the Progress of the People. 6 Vols. (Cassell, 1904).
Vol. 3. *Henry VIII to Elizabeth.*
Vol. 4. *James I to Anne.*
Vol. 5. *George I to Waterloo.*
Trevelyan, G. M., *Illustrated English Social History.* Vol. 3. The Eighteenth Century (Longmans, 1951).
Turberville, A. S., *Johnson's England;* an account of the life and manners of his Age. 2 Vols. (O.U.P., 1933).
Williams, P., *Life in Tudor England* (Batsford, 1964).

Transport and Communications
Harper, C. G., *Stage Coach and Mail in days of yore.* 2 Vols. (Chapman & Hall, 1903).
Lee, N. E., *Travel and Transport Through the Ages.* 2nd ed. (C.U.P., 1955).

Women
Camden, C., *The Elizabethan Woman; a Panorama of English Womanhood, 1540 to 1640* (Cleaver-Hume, 1952).
Clark, A., *Working Life of Women in the Seventeenth Century* (Routledge, 1919).
Fussell, G. E. and K. R., *The English Countrywoman; a Farmhouse Social History, A.D. 1500–1900* (Melrose, 1953).
Hole, C., *The English Housewife in the Seventeenth Century* (Chatto and Windus, 1953).
Stenton, Lady D. M., *The English Woman in History* (Allen and Unwin, 1957).
Williams, N., *Powder and Paint: a History of the Englishwoman's Toilet, Elizabeth I–Elizabeth II* (Longmans, 1957).

Dates	Kings and Queens of England and France	Famous Men	Great Events	Principal Buildings
1500	Henry VII and *Louis XII*	Hans Holbein *b.* 1497—P. Benvenuto Cellini *b.*—S.		Layer Marney Towers, Essex, 1500–25.
1501	. . . . . .	. . . . . .	Marriage of Arthur and Katherine of Arragon	East Barsham, Norfolk, 1501–15
1502	. . . . . .	. . . . . .	Marriage of Margaret and James IV of Scotland	
1503	. . . . . .	Sir Thomas Wyatt *b.*		
1504	. . . . . .	Grocyn—W.		
1506	. . . . . .	Colet, Dean of St. Paul's		
1508	. . . . . .	. . . . . .	. . . .	King's College, Cambridge
1509	Henry VIII, *m.* Katherine of Arragon; Anne Boleyn; Jane Seymour; Anne of Cleves; Katherine Howard; Katherine Parr			St. Paul's School founded
1510	. . . . . .	Erasmus—W.		
1511	. . . . . .	Sir Thomas More—W.	More writes *Utopia*	Westminster Abbey, Henry VII's Chapel
1513	. . . . . .	Cardinal Wolsey	Battle of Spurs, and Battle of Flodden	
1514	. . . . . .	. . . . . .	Wolsey made Archbishop	Hampton Court, 1514-40
1515	*Francis I*	Roger Ascham *b.*—W.		
1516	. . . . . .	. . . . . .	Publication of Erasmus' translation of the Testament, and More's *Utopia*	Henry VII's tomb
1518	. . . . . .	Palladio *b.*—A.		
1519	. . . . . .	Martin Luther	Luther's Objections	
1520	. . . . . .	. . . . . .	Field of Cloth of Gold	Compton Wynyates
1521	. . . . . .	. . . . . .	"Diet" at Worms	
1522	. . . . . .	. . . . . .	Luther publishes translation of Testament	
1523	. . . . . .	. . . . . .	. . . .	Sutton Place, Guildford, 1523-25
1526	. . . . . .	John Calvin		Hengrave Hall, Suffolk, 1526-38
1529	. . . . . .	. . . . . .	Fall of Wolsey	Ford's Hospital, Coventry
1530	. . . . . .	. . . . . .	Death of Wolsey	
1533	. . . . . .	. . . . . .	Divorce of Katherine	
1535	. . . . . .	. . . . . .	Death of More, Death of Erasmus. Execution of Anne Boleyn	
1536	. . . . . .	Robert Aske	Suppression of smaller Monasteries, 1536–40. Pilgrimage of Grace	
1539	. . . . . .	. . . . . .	Suppression of great Monasteries	
1540	. . . . . .	Stephen Gardiner	Fall of Cromwell	Lacock Abbey, Wilts.
1541	. . . . . .	. . . . . .	. . . .	Berkhamsted School founded
1542	. . . . . .	John Knox	War with Scotland. Battle of Solway Moss	
1543	. . . . . .	. . . . . .	War with France	
1544	. . . . . .	Cranmer		
1545	. . . . . .	. . . . . .	Confiscation of the Chantries	
1547	Edward VI and *Henry II*		Execution of Surrey	
1549	. . . . . .	Hugh Latimer		
1550	. . . . . .	Isaac Oliver	Peace with France and Scotland	Sherborne School founded
1551	. . . . . .	. . . . . .	. . . .	Shrewsbury School founded
1552	. . . . . .	Sir W. Raleigh *b.* Edmund Spenser *b.*—Pt.		Bedford School founded
1553	Mary		Lady Jane Grey proclaimed Queen	
1554	. . . . . .	Sir Philip Sidney *b.*—Pt.	Wyatt's Rebellion. Execution of Lady Jane Grey	
1555	. . . . . .	Cardinal Pole		
1556	. . . . . .	Ridley		
1557	. . . . . .	. . . . . .	. . . .	Repton School founded
1558	Elizabeth		Loss of Calais	Moreton Old Hall, Cheshire
1559	*Francis II*			
1560	*Charles IX*			
1561	*Regency of Catherine de Medici*	Francis Bacon *b.*—W.	Mary Stuart returns to Scotland	
1564	. . . . . .	William Shakespeare *b.*		
1565	. . . . . .	Christopher Marlowe *b.*—Pt.	Mary Stuart marries Darnley	Highgate School founded
1567	. . . . . .	. . . . . .	Murder of Darnley. Mary marries Bothwell	Longleat, Wilts.
1568	. . . . . .	. . . . . .	Mary imprisoned. Escapes to England	Rugby School founded
1569	. . . . . .	. . . . . .	Rising in the North	
1570	. . . . . .	. . . . . .	Pope excommunicates Elizabeth	Middle Temple Hall
1571	. . . . . .	. . . . . .	. . . .	Harrow School founded
1572	. . . . . .	Inigo Jones *b.*—A.		Burghley House, Northants
1573	. . . . . .	Ben Jonson *b.*—W.		
1574	*Henry III*			
1576	. . . . . .	. . . . . .	. . . .	Hardwick Hall
1577	. . . . . .	Peter Paul Rubens *b.*—P.	Drake sails round the world	
1580	. . . . . .	Franz Hals *b.*—P.		Montacute
1583	. . . . . .	. . . . . .	. . . .	Barlboro' House, Derbyshire
1584	. . . . . .	. . . . . .	. . . .	Uppingham School founded
1585	. . . . . .	. . . . . .	. . . .	Doddington Hall, Lincolnshire
1586	. . . . . .	. . . . . .	English expedition to the Netherlands	
1587	. . . . . .	Hawkins	Babington's Plot. Execution of Mary, Queen of Scots	
1588	. . . . . .	Drake	Arrival and defeat of the Spanish Armada	
1589	*Henry IV*	Sir Humphrey Gilbert	Publication of *Faerie Queene*	
1590	. . . . . .	Sir Martin Frobisher		
1591	. . . . . .	Robert Herrick *b.*—Pt.		
1593	. . . . . .	Izaak Walton *b.*—W.		Trinity College, Cambridge, Nevile's Court
1596	. . . . . .	. . . . . .	Attack on Cadiz	
1598	. . . . . .	Velasquez *b.* 1599—P.	Rebellion of Tyrone	Condover House, Shropshire
1599	. . . . . .	Sir A. Van Dyck *b.*—P.	Essex goes to Ireland	Broughton Castle, Oxon

A.=Architect. P.=Painter. Pt.=Poet. S.=Sculptor. W.=Writer.

3 Chart of the "Tudor" Period of Design, from 1500 to 1599

4 A Horseman at the Field of the Cloth of Gold

Chapter I
SIXTEENTH CENTURY

THE sixteenth century is a particularly interesting period, because it marks the change from the Middle Ages to the modern world; and this change, though not heralded by conquest, was in reality a far greater one than that which followed the coming of the Normans in 1066. We have already explained how William the Conqueror was responsible for the introduction into England of a new set of ideas; and in the same way the sixteenth century marked a general change of spirit which altered the whole outlook of the people and therefore the appearance of everyday things.

William's new ideas of 1066 were carefully grafted on to those of the Anglo-Saxons. He knit the country together by Feudalism. This, at its best, was a sound institution, based on the principle of service. The faith of Englishmen was not disturbed, but rather strengthened, by the work of such Norman bishops as Lanfranc and Anselm. Churchmen, said the nineteenth-century historian Froude, ruled the State, and "they were allowed to rule because they deserved to rule, and in the fullness of reverence kings and nobles bent before a power which was nearer to God than their own". Things were done and made, land was held, and lives lived more in common than is our practice nowadays; to borrow was thriftless, to lend usury. The Gothic cathedral was the product, not of one man, but of many, and still remains as one of the finest of human achievements.

Towards the end of the Middle Ages, however, people were becoming restless; the old standards were being overthrown; and nothing had yet arisen to take their place. In the old days men had worked together, and accepted the principle of service; for the latter the sixteenth century substituted that of competition. Men learned to sharpen their wits against their fellows. The individual begins to step out of the crowd and beckon to us.

Froude points the contrast as follows:

> In these times of ours, well-regulated selfishness is the recognized rule of action—every one of us is expected to look out first for himself, and take care of his own interests. At the time I speak of, the Church ruled the State with the authority of a conscience, and self-interest, as a motive of action, was only named to be abhorred.

This was written in 1867, and may not be so true now as it was then. From the sixteenth century, nevertheless, we have inherited both some of our modern vices and many of our virtues; and, if it were possible for a boy or girl who reads this book to meet a boy who went to the sixteenth-century school(20), they would find they had a great deal in common, not only in the things they used, but what is more important, in the things they thought about. But if our readers could be taken back to the Eton that Henry VI founded, the position would be reversed. They would find themselves confronted with an entirely different outlook.

SOCIAL LIFE

To understand the sixteenth-century world, we must first understand how society was then divided up. William Harrison in 1577 split the people of England into four classes: gentlemen, that is princes, lords, men of title, and squires or country

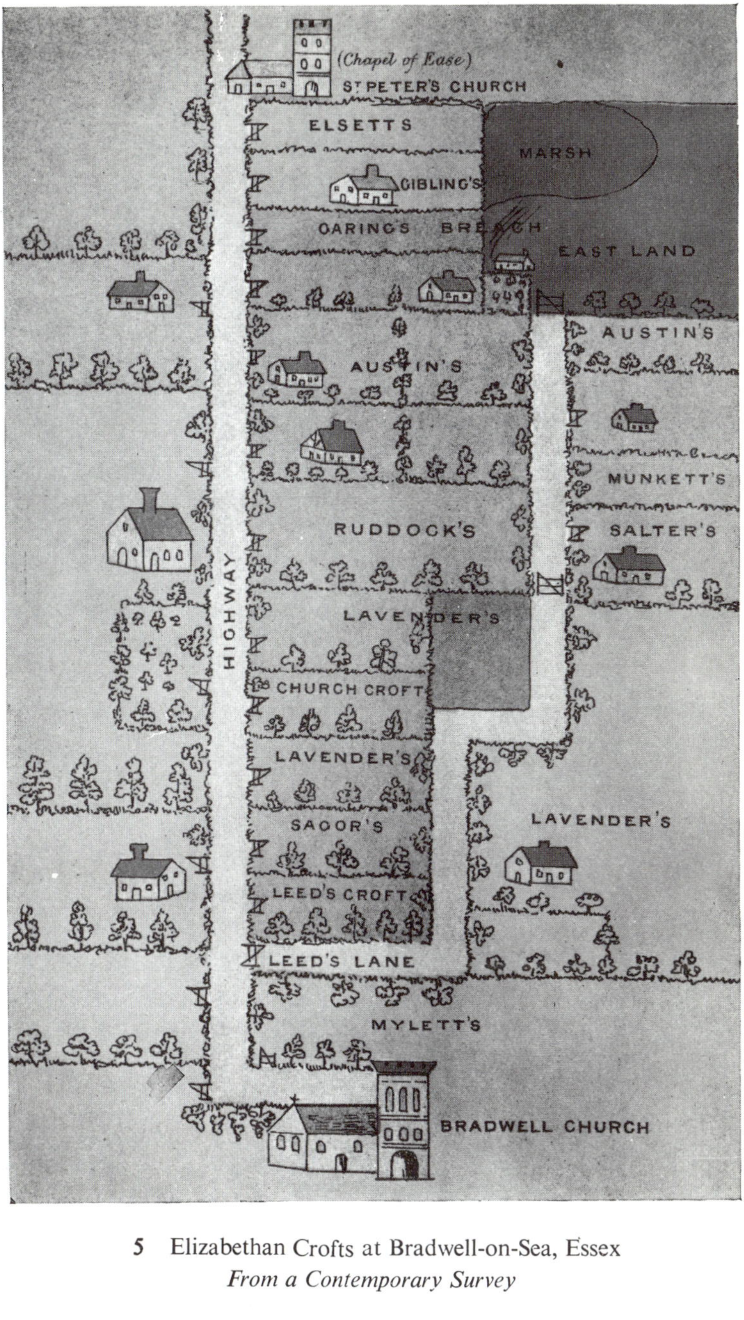

5 Elizabethan Crofts at Bradwell-on-Sea, Essex
From a Contemporary Survey

gentlemen holding land; citizens or burgesses, the great new English middle class, traders at home and abroad, who were rapidly gaining in importance; the farmers and yeomen, cultivators and producers of the goods sold and of foodstuffs; and lastly the artificers and labourers who worked for hire. These men, formerly villeins, were nearly all free men by the end of the reign of Henry VIII. Land was changing hands; the suppression of the monasteries and the transference of large tracts of land to the Crown, and thence by gift or purchase to new owners, led to diminished cultivation.

The sixteenth-century landowner, whose land was a commercial asset, not a personal inheritance, was often tempted by the growth of the wool trade to graze sheep on his acres, instead of cultivating the soil, thereby halving the labour needed and throwing many out of work. At the same time, rents began to be paid in money rather than in labour. This later caused many difficulties; for, whereas a man could pay his landlord by working certain hours for him, it was vastly more difficult to get outside work with pay in order to find the money for the rent. Elizabeth, to help the cause of the labourers, passed a law that no cottage was to be built in less than four acres of land, so as to ensure that cottagers had some dependable means of livelihood. Many a poor man planted on this land cabbages, radishes, turnips, parsnips, carrots, melons, pompons (pumpkins), and kept a pig or cow; "by which," as William Harrison says, "he and his poor household liveth as their principal food, sith they can do no better". A collection of Elizabethan small-holdings is shown in fig. 5, which is taken from a contemporary map of part of the parish of Bradwell-on-Sea, Essex.

Harrison describes the growing evils brought on by increasing trade. He says that in the past men made goods and sold them, but that now middlemen in the markets eat up the grower's profits; that purveyors purchase butter, eggs, cheese, pigs, capons, hens, chickens, hogs, and bacon in one market, and suffer their wives to sell them in another market or to the poulterers of London. "Whereby also I gather," he writes, "that the maintenance of a superfluous number of dealers in most trades is one of the greatest causes why the prices of things become excessive."

Markets were held once a week in all towns and all things

6 Vagabonds, 1609

needed for household use were sold and bought there; large fairs were usually held once or twice a year.

Shops were increasing rapidly in the towns, and usually consisted of a single room level with the street, the shutter of which let down to form a counter, while a sign hung above denoted the trade. At first the room behind was often used for the making of the goods to be sold; but, as time went on, the shop became the place where goods were "brought" to be sold, rather than "made" to be sold.

As the towns grew, new houses were erected with little regard to space or place, and the streets became narrow and overcrowded. Generally ill-paved, with all the house rubbish thrown out into them, and ill-lit except where the wealthier inhabitants were obliged by law to hang out lanthorns, the streets cannot have been pleasant to walk in. During the latter half of the sixteenth century, scavengers and dust-carts were appointed to clear the rubbish in the streets, and a number of leading citizens were bound to keep leather buckets of water and great hooks in readiness to fight fires. Two force-pumps, worked with wheels, were also set up to supply water. Fire was an ever-present danger in narrow congested streets of wooden or timber-framed houses.

Distress in the country drove labourers towards the town; and overcrowding grew and, with it, slums. Parts of London became plague-spots of poverty; filth and vice were rampant. A law was passed that one house should be occupied by only one family; but it proved impossible to enforce in the human rabbit-warrens that were springing up. Another law forbade the erection of buildings on hitherto unoccupied parts of the city. But these measures were powerless to stem the influx of the unemployed and unemployable; or to prevent them from herding together in the most congested neighbourhoods. Citizens out after dark dared not venture unaccompanied, and carried lanterns and swords if they were obliged to leave their homes. For footpads and cut-throats haunted the streets; while, throughout the countryside, the unemployed joined together in marauding bands, pilfering, robbing, and terrifying whole villages.

The nursery rhyme "The beggars are coming to London Town"(7) was then no mere jingle, but described a genuine threat. As often as a horde of beggars was reported to be approaching, respectable citizens on the outskirts hastened to put up their shutters, barricaded themselves in their houses and barred their stables and their cowsheds. Edward VI was so moved by a sermon of Bishop Ridley concerning the plight of the great poverty-stricken hordes in parts of London, that he wrote to the Lord Mayor, through whom a committee was formed to inquire into the matter; and finally three houses were founded, "Graie Friars", now Christ's Hospital for poor children, St. Thomas of Southwark, and St. Bartholomew in Smithfield for at least two hundred diseased persons; to which was added Bridewell, a prison for the correction of idlers and

7 A Horde of Beggars Invading a Town
From an Engraving by Weidetz, 1535

vagabonds. In 1569 such a host of beggars converged on London that the Corporation appointed a special force of beadles, who were to send off the able-bodied to Bridewell, the diseased to St. Bartholomew's Hospital, and the children to Christ's Hospital.

COSTUME

Having considered the social life of the period, and how the classes were divided, let us now turn to everyday things and examine the general appearance of the age. Fig. 2 shows the costume of the time. In Vol. I we saw that the middle part of the fifteenth century was a period of great extravagance, and that clothes were often designed to distort rather than clothe the figure. Men's garments either trailed on the ground or were cut excessively short; head-dresses were monstrous, and shoes so long and pointed that they were fastened up to the knee. Each period has its own type of design, which runs through everything made during that epoch. The detail of fifteenth-century architecture was reflected in dress; and, when the Renaissance came, the pointed forms of the Gothic period gave way to fuller and rounder shapes.

8 "Fforstaller and Regrator of Markets and Feyres and Vittellars", 1509[1]

In the reign of Edward IV the fifteenth-century spirit of extravagance began to die out, and dress became gradually simpler. This continued until the end of the reign of Henry VII, to which period belong the first two figures of our illustration (2). Observe the lady's dress. The surcoat has disappeared, and her gown is simple. The bodice is cut square to show the white partelet at the neck, and fits the figure closely. The sleeves are full and the skirt is gathered into the waist with a jewelled belt. Under-sleeves were worn, probably attached separately. The high head-dress has given place to a flat kerchief-like covering. The man standing beside her wears a flat velvet cap

[1] Fforstaller was one who bought goods on the way to market; regrator one who created a corner in goods in the market.

and a tunic and hose, beneath a loose full gown with hanging sleeves. His shoes, too, are comparatively simple in shape. The figures illustrate a style in its intermediate stage, before it has had time to become exaggerated.

9 Children of 1563

The second lady belongs to the next reign, that of Henry VIII. Her bodice is stiffened, like her skirt, which is open in front to show a richly embroidered kirtle. Her hanging sleeves are fastened back to display the beautiful brocaded lining. The under-sleeves are slit from elbow to wrist and puffed with lawn. For the first time we see ruffles at the wrist. The kerchief has been altered and the ends are caught up on to the top, forming a three-cornered head-dress.

The interchange of courtesies between Henry VIII and the French Court led to a great influx of French fashions, and men's dress became extremely rich and heavy. Every garment worn by the second man in this illustration is wonderfully slashed, laced, and embroidered. The outer coat is of velvet or heavy silk, and is lined with fur; the short breeches or trunks, hidden by his doublet, are of the same material. The sleeves are bolstered and slashed. The doublet or inner coat is also richly trimmed; and, though in this illustration it is closed, it was often opened to display a richly embroidered shirt or French chemay beneath. The slashed shoes are very broad. The flat velvet cap is plumed, and the gentleman's hair is closely cut, following the French fashion rigorously enforced at the Court of Henry VIII.

The third couple belong to the reign of Queen Elizabeth. Little by little, dresses grew stiffer, more ungainly and more heavily ornamented; until a climax of elaboration was reached in the shape of the monstrous wheeled farthingale, which came into fashion towards the latter half of Elizabeth's reign, and lasted well on into the reign of James I. This farthingale consisted of a very full gathered skirt which was stretched out over a

10 A Physician, 1562

large hoop round the hips, thence falling straight to the ground—a very ungainly and ugly fashion. Bodices were stiff and peaked, and among wealthy women embroidered with gold and jewels (2). Ruffs were of Spanish origin. They began as cambric collars (notice the second man's costume), and became larger and more elaborately pleated and wired, until they resembled those worn by the third couple in the picture. But the ruffs we show are not extreme examples; sometimes they were larger and much more curious in form. Special sticks were used to plait these ruffs, called pokesticks. An alternative fashion was the wearing of large, fan-like collars, made in lawn or cambric, materials first brought to England during the reign of Queen Elizabeth. These fan-shaped collars reached immense proportions, two or three layers of cambric being used, each wired to stand stiffly up and away from the head. Examples are shown on the ladies in the hall (38).

An interesting account of Queen Elizabeth's clothing as a child is given in a letter from Lady Bryan, found among State papers of the period. After Anne Boleyn's disgrace and death, the Princess Elizabeth was put under the care of Lady Bryan, and was apparently neglected by her father, Henry VIII; for Lady Bryan complains that the Princess

> hath neither gown, nor kirtle, nor peticoat, nor no manner of linen, nor foresmocks [pinafores], nor kerchiefs, nor rails [night-dresses], nor body stitchets [corsets], nor handkerchiefs, nor sleeves, nor mufflers, nor biggens [caps].

We must remember that children wore just the same clothing as their elders; and the inventory of a child's needs would be nealry identical with that of a grown-up person. Many tales could be told of Elizabeth's gowns when she had become Queen; and, if she lacked clothes in her youth, she certainly made up for it in later years. On her death, she is said to have left behind a thousand dresses in her wardrobe.

An account of the dress that Mary Queen of Scots, Elizabeth's great rival, wore to her execution throws further light on feminine fashions of the day:

> Then did she apparel herself after this manner, in borrowed hair, having on her head a dressing of lawn edged with bone lace and above that a vail [veil] of the same, bowed out with weir [wire], and her cuffs suitable; and about her neck, a pomander chain and an Agnus Dei hanging at a black ribband, a crucifix in her hand, a pair of beads at her girdle with a golden cross at the end. Her uppermost gown was of black satin, printed, training upon the ground, with long hanging sleeves trimmed with akorn buttons of jet and pearl, the sleeves over her arms being cut, to give sight to a pair of purple velvet underneath; her kirtle, as her gown, was of black printed satin: her bodice of crimson satin unlaced in the back, the skirt being of crimson velvet: her stockings of worsted, watchet, clocked, and edged at the top with silver, and under them a pair of white: her shoes of Spanish leather with the rough side outward.

The gown referred to here would be a garment often worn at this time, and sometimes called a mandeville. One can still be seen at the Victoria and Albert Museum, South Kensington. It was a long mantle or tunic open and unfastened in the front, with long unused sleeves, the arm coming through an opening by the shoulder.

To return, however, to fig. 2. The third lady wears a feathered hat, and under it the small French hood brought into fashion by Henry VIII's wife, Anne of Cleves, and still worn by Elizabethan ladies. The hair, as a rule, was elaborately curled and dressed high, and was often covered with a jewelled caul or net. Many laws were in force regarding dress; and, unless their husbands could prove themselves to be gentlemen by descent, citizens' wives were obliged to wear white knitted caps of woollen yarn. In the reign of Queen Mary, all London apprentices wore blue gowns in winter and blue cloaks in summer, with breeches of white broadcloth and flat caps. Servants might not wear gowns that fell below the calf of the leg.

The third man in our illustration wears a peaked doublet, of the same shape as that worn by the lady. Like that of his companion, it is elaborately ornamented, and the sleeves are padded. He wears trunks—the very short stuffed breeches—

11 An apprentice going to draw water, 1572

trunk hose which reach to above the knee, and hose or stockings. These trunk hose are the beginning of the breeches of later days, and mark the end of the long chausses of medieval times. A later type of Elizabethan dress can be seen in fig. 38. Here some of the men wear no trunks, but trunk hose and hose, the former padded until they resemble bolsters (see also fig. 51). Later still, the padding was omitted, but the fullness retained; and they were then called galligaskins, gradually becoming narrower until they developed into the full breeches worn by the Cavaliers. Short cloaks to the hip were largely worn, and often made of perfumed leather. Note that the gentleman's shoes have heels, and more closely resemble modern shoes than any we have yet studied.

Fig. 12 illustrates a very interesting unbleached linen stocking from a private collection. The material is cut on the cross, which means that the warp threads do not run vertically up and down on the stocking, which is consequently a little more elastic. The stocking is shaped and seamed at the back, and stitched with green silk. The sole is cut larger than the foot, as a separate piece, and brought up and gathered to the shape of the foot, and sewn

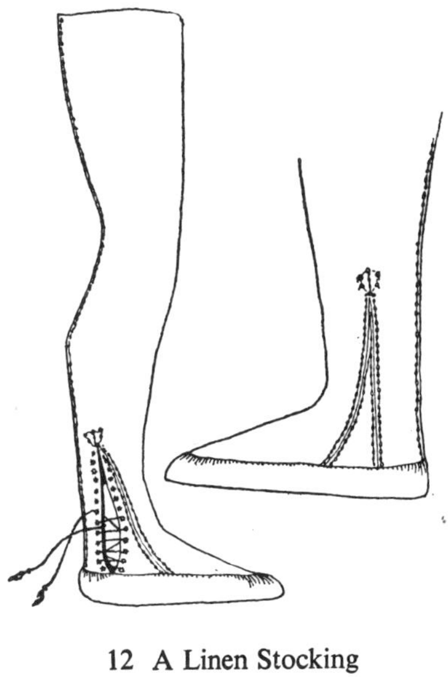

12 A Linen Stocking

to the upper portion. Gussets are inserted in each side, the seams having ornamental stitchery of green silk. On the outside, the back seam of the gusset is left open to make the ankle large enough for the passage of the foot, and the gusset then closed by drawing up a green silk cord, through green silk eyelet holes, and tied at the top, which is finished with a clock to prevent the material splitting. The clock still remains as an ornament on some stockings of the present day.

THE NEW LEARNING AND VOYAGES OF DISCOVERY

During this period of rapid social change, what advances were being made in thought? Among other important events recorded on our fifteenth-century chart was the conquest of Constantinople by the Turks in 1453. From that centre of ancient learning fugitive scholars scattered all over Europe, with the result that classical studies were revived, and the literary masterpieces of Greece and Rome were translated, imitated and widely discussed. Caxton started printing at Westminster in 1476; Grocyn, a Fellow of New College, gave classical lectures at Oxford. It is difficult for us to understand today how marvellous this revival of learning must have seemed to people who knew only medieval literature. The two traditions are as different from one another as Roman characters are from Gothic script—the latter, decorative but hard to read; the former, beautifully clear and simple.

Erasmus, born in 1467, was first a monk, but obtained release from his vows from Julius II. He came to England in 1497 and met Sir Thomas More and Dean Colet. The influence of these men was to be tremendous, and they were all learned, sincere, and good men. "I have given up my whole soul to Greek learning," said Erasmus, "and as soon as I get any money I shall buy Greek books—and then I shall buy some clothes"; and, concerning More, he demanded, "When did Nature mould a temper more gentle, endearing, and happy than the temper of Thomas More?" We must remember that, although these men wished to reform the Church, they had no desire to break away from its teaching; the course that the Reformation eventually took was repugnant to them; and Sir Thomas More laid down his life rather than surrender his religious principles.

Had men been wise enough to accept Sir Thomas More as

the champion of the Reformation, we can judge from the pages of *Utopia*,[1] which he wrote in 1516, of the kindlier spirit that might have been brought to bear on the problems of the Church.

> It should be lawfull [we read in *Utopia*] for everie man to favoure and folow what religion he would, and that he mighte do the best he could to bring other to his opinion, so that he did it peaceablie, gentelie, and soberlie, without hastie and contentious rebuking and invehing against other. If he could not by faire and gentle speche induce them unto his opinion yet he should use no kinde of violence, and refraine from displeasaunte and seditious woordes.

Erasmus was rendered miserable by having to stand between the two extreme parties; like More and Colet, he saw that the Church needed reformation, but hated the methods by which it was accomplished.

THE ELIZABETHAN NAVY

Meanwhile, besides rediscovering the classical past, men were beginning to look towards the New World. In Vol. I we have discussed the importance of sea-power during the Middle Ages; and in the sixteenth century it was the English Navy that enabled us to hold the Channel and defeat the Spanish Armada. Froude's *English Seamen of the Sixteenth Century* gives a magnificent picture of our naval progress. Columbus had discovered America in 1492; and Spain had laid the foundations of empire that stretched across the ocean. Though challenged by England, she continued to rule the seas, until the great trial of strength came, with the launching of the Spanish Armada, in 1588. England owed that momentous victory to her gallant and experienced sailors and their superior seamanship.

They had learned much from their voyages to the New World. England, like other European nations, had been deeply stirred by the discovery of America; and fabulous tales were told of the wealth to be obtained there. Fig. 13 shows what a hazy idea the old navigators had of the shape of the New World, and the terrors that they imagined lying in wait for them across the Atlantic.

The Revival of Learning led to an intense interest and curiosity

[1] *Utopia* deals with More's conception of the Ideal State.

13 The New World

From Ptolemy's *Geographia Universalis*, 1540

in other people's doings: a spirit of adventure was in the air. Wise old Henry VII understood this, and the necessity for being up and doing. The first English expedition to America sailed in 1497, under John Cabot. Henry built the *Regent*, and the *Sovereign*, both larger and more powerful than any ships that had gone before. The *Great Harry*, launched in 1514, was the wonder of her day: and Henry VIII, assisted by Wolsey, continued the good work of his father, and should probably be regarded as the founder of the Royal Navy. Before this, ships had been provided by the Cinque Ports. Henry greatly encouraged the seamen of his time, and William Hawkins sailed under his flag to Guinea. Later, in Elizabeth's time, his son, Sir John Hawkins, engaged in the slave trade, and opened the route to the West Indies. In 1577 Drake sailed out of Plymouth Sound in the *Pelican*, of only 120 tons, the *Elizabeth*, of 80 tons, and two sloops, of 50 and 30 tons. He sailed clean round the world, causing the Spaniards grave alarm; they recognised that a nation capable of producing such sailors might soon become a dangerous rival. Thus were the sailors trained who out-manœuvred and defeated the Armada.

SHIPBUILDING

In Vol. I we described how the Crusaders were impressed by the development of Eastern shipping, and how, during the fifteenth century, northern shipwrights adopted the lateen, or leg-of-mutton, sail. This innovation enabled them to sail a little closer to the wind, and made it easier to work their ships. In fig. 14 the right-hand side of the diagram represents the best that a medieval boat could do, fitted only with square sails. She was at her *best* with the wind right aft. The left-hand side of the diagram illustrates a cutter or hoy rig, which is fore and aft and descended from the lateen. Here the navigator was not hampered by yards and shrouds, and the boat could get to within four

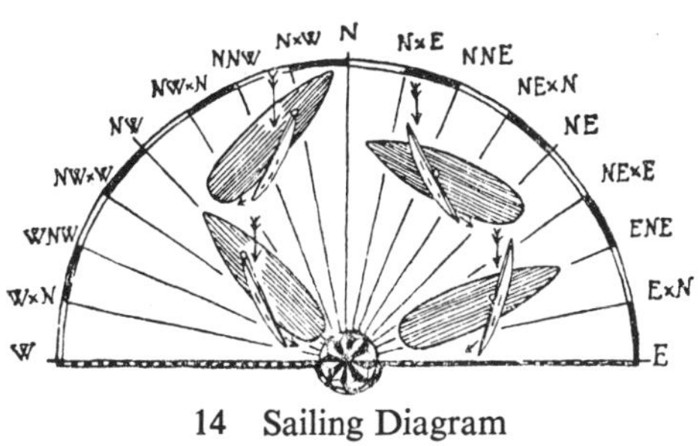

14 Sailing Diagram

15 A Mediterranean Galley

points of the wind. But the fore and aft was at its *worst* with the wind due aft; a combination of the two rigs was what the old seafarers aimed at. They did not at once develop the lateen into triangular head-sails, stay-sails, and spanker: this was done gradually, as we shall see in the illustrations. What they did, in the fifteenth and sixteenth centuries, was to adapt the lateen to the mizzen and Bonaventure mizzen; and the purpose must have been to allow them to change over from one tack to the other more readily. They can scarcely have hoped to lay their ships closer to the wind, since the hulls were not high enough in the bows to make the attempt desirable.

Fig. 15 illustrates a Mediterranean galley, drawn from a model at the Science Museum at South Kensington, which is said to have belonged to the Knights of Malta. Though later in date than the sixteenth century, it may be taken as typical of the Eastern galley, which influenced the design of the Elizabethan galleon. Here we must explain that galleon meant a man-of-war; gallease was a smaller boat, like the frigate later on. The galley illustrated has a beak head, used for ramming, and a forecastle.

The main deck is equipped with twenty-two long sweeps on each side for use in calm weather, manned by slaves, who sat on benches, several pulling at each sweep. Up and down the deck, a raised gangway ran between the benches, whence the overseers could wield their whips against any slave who did not pull his weight.

In Kingsley's *Westward Ho!* Salvation Yeo recounts his experiences as a Spanish galley-slave to Sir Richard Grenville and Amyas Leigh:

> I must have two hundred stripes in the public place, and then go to the galleys for seven years. And there, gentlemen, ofttimes I thought that it had been better for me to have been burned at once and for all: but you know as well as I, what a floating hell of heat and cold, hunger and thirst, stripes and toil, is every one of those accursed craft.

The build of the hull of the galley influenced ship-design for many years; and we have already discussed the influence of the lateen, or leg-of-mutton, sails which are shown furled on the foremast, mainmast, and mizzen. The length of the galley we have drawn is given as 165 feet, its breadth as 22 feet.

Fig. 16 shows an Elizabethan galleon with a beak head closely resembling that of the galley, forecastle, and high poop. The amusing little turrets, and the ornament, show how closely related was the architecture of the sea to the construction of buildings on dry land. The open stern galley is a new feature. So far as rig is concerned, we now have a spritsail on the bowsprit. The foremast and mainmast are square rigged: and the most interesting features are the lateen sails on the mizzen and Bonaventure mizzen. Netting was used over the waist of the ship as a defence against boarders. Sometimes the ends of the bowsprit and the yards were provided with hooks to catch in and cut through an enemy's rigging at close quarters. The sails are shown with detachable bonnets laced on, which could be removed instead of reefing. At this period topmasts were arranged so that they could be lowered.

Fig. 17 is a drawing of the *Ark Royal*, from a print in the British Museum. This fine boat was built for Sir Walter Raleigh in 1587, but afterwards sold to Queen Elizabeth for £5,000. She was the flagship of the fleet that defeated the Armada and, as

16 An Elizabethan Galleon

such, is entitled to our respectful consideration. Her tonnage was 800, and her crew numbered 400. In 1608 she was rebuilt and named the *Anne Royal*. Froude gives us a picture of the memorable council of war held in the main cabin of the *Ark*, on Sunday afternoon, August 8th, 1588. The Armada had been chased up the Channel and, if left undisturbed, would have recovered and been ready to embark Parma and his troops at Dunkirk. So "Howard, Drake, Seymour, Hawkins, Martin Frobisher, and two or three others met to consult, knowing that on them at that moment were depending the liberties of England".

The hull of the *Ark Royal* was still on galley lines: and here we must remember how the term quarter-deck came about. In an Elizabethan ship, seen from the bows, the forecastle was followed by the waist, itself followed by the half-deck; the next portion was called the quarter-deck, because it occupied roughly one quarter of the space: the remaining portion aft was the poop. The rig is the same as that of the galleon; but the mizzens are more liberally provided with lateen sails.

Continuing the wise policy of her father and grandfather, Queen Elizabeth encouraged trade. She granted the first charter to the East India Company in 1600, and so laid the foundation of our Eastern Empire. There were only five ships in the first fleet of the Company that sailed; and the largest of these, by name the *Dragon*, was only of 600 tons, with a crew of 202.

Hakluyt, in his famous book of voyages, writing of English trade in the sixteenth century, tells us that the ships of London, Southampton, and Bristol traded with Sicily, Tripoli, and Beirut in Syria, carrying these

> fine kerseys[1] [cloth] of divers colours, coarse kerseys, white western dozens, cottons, certain cloths called statutes and others called cardinal whites, and calf-skins, which were well sold in Sicily.

They brought home silks, camlets, rhubarb, malmseys, muscadels, and other wines, sweet oils, cotton, wood, Turkey carpets, galls, pepper, cinnamon, and other spices.

17 The *Ark Royal*

[1] From Kersey, the cloth village in Suffolk.

Hakluyt also describes the voyages of discovery to which we have referred upon an earlier page, and the dangers encountered by the men and ships engaged in them. Sir Hugh Willoughby was among the first explorers to lose their lives seeking for the North-east or North-west Passage to India. The ships themselves were often severely tried; and Hakluyt informs us that the sixteenth-century sailormen found that, in tropic seas,

> a kind of worm is bred which many times pierceth and eateth through the strongest oak that is; therefore that the mariners might be free and safe from this danger, they cover a piece of the keel of the ship with thin sheets of lead.

THE NEW SCHOOLS

Among the greatest monuments of the sixteenth century are the schools that it founded or re-established. They include St. Paul's (1509), Berkhamsted (1541), Sherborne (1550), Shrewsbury (1551), Bedford, one of the sixteen schools founded by Edward VI (1552), Repton (1557), Highgate (1565), Rugby (1567), Harrow (1571), Uppingham (1584), and many others.

The Tudors, who were themselves very well educated, determined that their subjects should enjoy a similar privilege; often the buildings they provided are still serving the same purpose.

There is a general tendency, however, to assume that grammar schools did not exist before this time, and that education was in the hands of the monks. This is quite untrue. We saw in Vol. I how the Benedictine monastery had a training school for novices who wished to become monks, and sometimes another in connection with the almonry, where poor boys were trained for the choir. The precentor taught them singing: and such choir schools were the elementary schools of the day. Where there was a town, it is probable that the townsmen and guilds had their own grammar school. The foundations of secular canons, as at Chichester, Wells, York, Southwell, Lincoln, Hereford,

18 A boy of 1509

and Beverley, took more interest in education than did the monastic foundations; and they maintained schools, or licensed masters to keep them. Generally, there was a theological school, under the chancellor, a grammar school, under a master appointed by the chancellor, and a choir school, under the precentor. On pages 48 and 49, we describe the difference between secular and monastic foundations.

Collegiate churches, such as Winchester and Eton, carried on the good work. William of Wykeham founded Winchester, as early as 1382, for "seventy poor and needy scholars, clerks, living collegewise therein and studying and becoming proficient in grammaticals or the art, faculty, or science of grammar". A bird's-eye view of the college is shown at fig. 21. Wykeham also founded New College, Oxford; and boys went there on leaving Winchester—at an earlier age than now. Eton came into being in 1440: and Henry VI planned it to consist of provost, ten priests, four clerks, six chorister boys, and "twenty-five poor and needy scholars to learn grammar there". The Eton boys of the fifteenth century said the Matins of the Blessed Virgin while making the beds in the dormitories before five o'clock in the morning. King's College, Cambridge, was founded in conjunction with Eton.

Chantry schools were attached to a church, where the priest taught children, as well as singing Masses for the founder. The chantries were dissolved in 1547.

Grammar schools were sometimes founded in association with colleges, as at Queen's College, Oxford, where the boys served as choristers, but had masters of their own, although they dined in hall with the scholars.

During the Middle Ages the schools taught grammar, logic, and rhetoric, which were called the Trivium, and arithmetic, music, geometry, astronomy, known as the Quadrivium. Teaching was mainly oral, since, before printing became general, books were far too expensive to be used for classwork. A boy was taught to hold his own in wordy disputation, and to argue on such abstruse questions as—How many angels could sit on a pin's point? We still talk of a Senior Wrangler, and the term was originally applied to a scholar who could hold his own in disputation. Medieval education was severely practical; it fitted a man to be a cleric or a lawyer, but denied him the wider interests later supplied by the Renaissance. The patron saints of schoolboys were St. Katherine of Egypt and St. Nicholas of Myra.

St. Paul's School, founded by Dean Colet for 153 boys, was established "for the continuation of a certain school in the cemetery of St. Paul's". The boys were to be taught

> All way in good litterature with laten and greke and goode auctours such as have the veray Romayne eliquence joyned withe wysdome, specially Cristyn auctours that wrote theyre wysdome withe clene and chast laten other in verse or in prose.

Wolsey founded a school at Ipswich, from which boys went up to Christ Church, Oxford. The City Companies played their part; the Mercers were named as trustees of Dean Colet's School: and the Fishmongers are still trustees of the school at Holt founded by Sir John Gresham in 1555. The new schools were notably democratic. At the sixteenth-century Harrow, the pupils were to be of "the poorest sort, if they shall be apt".

Berkhamsted School was founded by another Dean of St. Paul's, John Incent, in 1541, who arranged for

19 An Elizabethan Dame School

20 The Old Hall, Berkhamsted School

> one Free Scole within the towne of Berkhampstedde, of one mete man being a scolemaster, and one other mete man being an ussher for the techyng of children in grammar frely, withoute any exaccion or request of money for the techyng of the same children.

"Th'ole building", declared an Elizabethan writer, "is so strong an faire that the like Grammar Schoole for that point is not to be seene in the whole realme of England." Large central windows mark the hall. On the right-hand side lived "one mete man being a scolemaster", as his successor does today; on the left was the house of the "other mete man being an ussher". Boys who boarded at the school probably lived in their houses.

The interior of the school hall is shown in fig. 20, but some restoration has been necessary. The hall still remained the central feature of almost any secular building; here the boys were taught, sitting in classes round the room rather as at a modern Sunday school; and there were no separate classrooms. They worked long hours, from six till eleven in the morning, and one to six in the afternoon in the summer, and two hours less in winter. It was not all book-work, though; boys and girls were trained in hawking, hunting, archery, and playing upon the lute and virginal, as a regular part of their education. One of the school orders at Harrow ran: "You shall allow your child at all times bow-shafts, bow-strings, and a bracer [sleeve guard] to exercise shooting."

Holidays were few. At Shrewsbury the boys were allowed eighteen days at Christmas, twelve at Easter, and nine at Whitsuntide.

Roger Ascham, tutor of Lady Jane Grey and Queen Elizabeth, must be remembered as one of the first of the great English schoolmasters. His book, *The Scholemaster*, published in 1570, marked an important advance in education.

COLLEGES

The early college (21) closely resembled a school or, for that matter, a house of the period. In fact, the Oxford or Cambridge college of today affords an excellent example of the medieval method of house-planning which obtained until Elizabeth's time. There was the hall with its screens, the buttery, and kitchen. A chapel was included later, but did not form part of the early medieval colleges, where the students attended the parish church. The hall originally served for common-room as well. All this part of the plan usually occupied one side of a square quadrangle, around which were later grouped the men's rooms, like the lodgings in an Elizabethan house. College rooms were used by more than one man: the larger as a dormitory for perhaps four men, and the smaller as a study. On the side of the

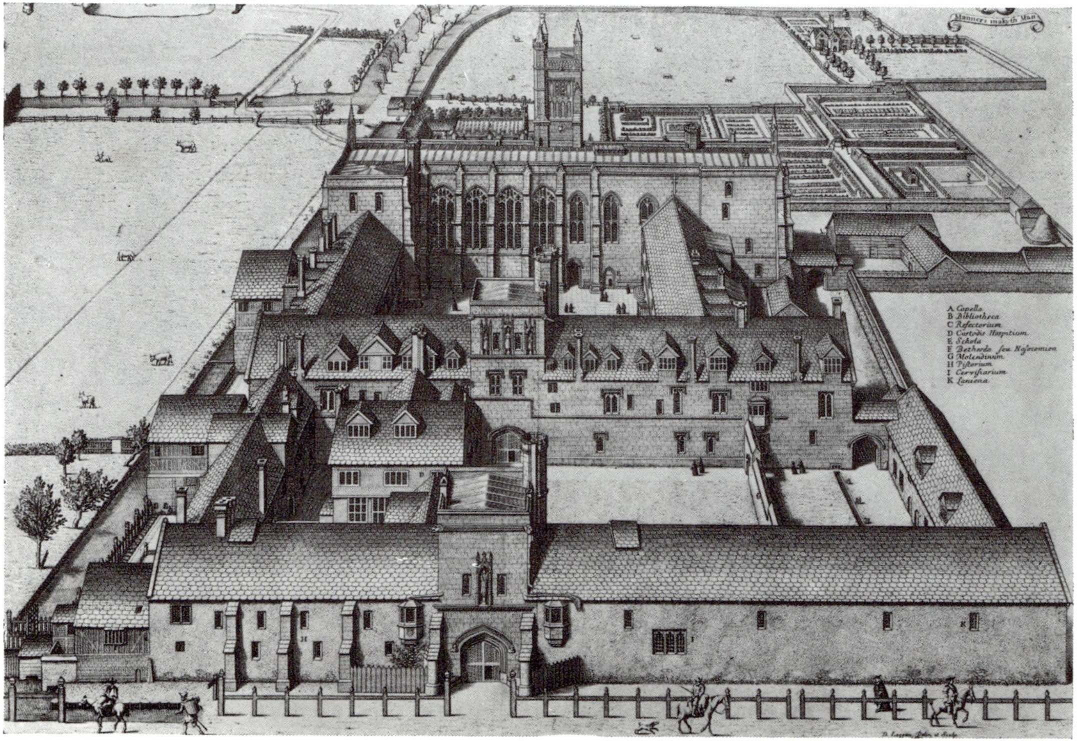

21 Winchester College

From an Engraving by David Loggan, 1675

quadrangle opposite the hall stood the gatehouse, as in the house plan; and here the porter mounted guard; while, as an additional precaution, the warden's lodging was generally over and around the gateway. All colleges, of course, did not follow this plan; we find all sorts of delightful variations of the idea, and skilful adaptations of it to suit the peculiarities of different sites. We hope some of our readers may look forward to becoming architects; and them we advise to consult our plan of a Benedictine monastery, Vol. I, Chapter I. It supplied the pattern that was gradually developed, to reach its last stage in the sixteenth century.

CATHEDRALS

In Vol. I we described the constitution of a Benedictine monastery, and pointed out that many of the great churches that we now call cathedrals were, in pre-Reformation times, the private chapels of the monasteries. But, if the abbot happened to be a bishop as well, and the church contained his throne, then it became a cathedral. After Henry VIII had dissolved the monasteries, the monastic cathedral was administered by a chapter of secular canons; and these were said to be of the New Foundation. But during the Middle Ages, too, there had been non-monastic cathedrals, administered always by secular canons, like Wells, Exeter, and Salisbury; and these were called as of the Old Foundation.

Secular clergy have existed from the earliest times. They were the parish priests, and canons of cathedral and collegiate churches. They lived in the world, had their own houses, and frequently, in very early days, were married. They did not take the vows of poverty, chastity, and obedience, as the monks did, but agreed, as now, to obey the law of the Church. About the time of the Conquest, the canons at Wells and Exeter began to live in a community that resembled a monastic brotherhood; but the custom never became very general.

In the old days canons were resident; and it is this fact that makes Wells Cathedral so interesting; there we find the bishop's palace, deanery, and houses for the canons and vicars, and much more accommodation than would have been required for a monastic cathedral. Wells has changed very little since pre-Reformation days. Because it belonged to the Old Foundation, it was never altered as were so many of the monastic cathedrals in Henry VIII's time, when the monks' quarters were pulled down. Canons of the Old Foundation, who were not resident, appointed vicars to take their place; and these must not be confounded with the minor canons in cathedrals founded by Henry VIII.

Confusion often arises between the names canon and prebendary; but, in reality, they mean the same. A man is canon by virtue of being a member of the body of the dean and chapter; prebendary, as the holder of a certain canonry, or prebend (*præbenda*), or separate estate.

Both Winchester and Eton were founded as collegiate churches, with a chapter, or college, of clergy who made education one of their duties.

HOUSES AND HOUSEHOLDERS

Fig. 22 depicts a timber-framed house of the Elizabethan period. Houses had been built in this way from the earliest times; and where such a method of construction is adopted, we know that the district must at one moment have been rich in trees. The old workmen always used local materials, and by so doing produced buildings that harmonised beautifully with their surroundings; a house built of local stone, bricks, or timber, seems to fit in and tune with the countryside, and does so because it is so closely related to Mother Earth. Slates, for instance, look out of key if imported into a tile country. So, wherever sturdy oaks flourished, you find timber-framed houses. The oaks were felled, placed over a pit, and cut up by two men using a long two-handled saw. The man on top of the log was the top sawyer; the one in the pit beneath, the bottom sawyer. Smaller stuff was squared and faced up with a beautiful tool called an adze, which has now nearly gone out of use. In shape it was like a garden hoe, with a longer and sharper blade, and shorter handle. The man using it stood on his work and chopped off thick shavings towards his foot; a skilful craftsman could face up oak to nearly the same smoothness as if he had employed a plane; but the general surface was more undulating. This was a great advantage. The old builders knew that oak was fibrous, and the more closely the fibre was followed the better; and this the adze did. When one of the writers

22 A Timber-framed House

Drawing founded on Rumwood Court, Langley, Kent

23 The Framework of a Kentish Timber House
Drawn by Sydney R. Jones

was young, there were old workmen who, for a wager, would take off one boot, put a penny under the big toe, bring their adze down, and nick the edge of the penny without damaging the toe that held it. This gives some idea of what the dexterous handling of tools can mean.

In the construction of a timber-framed house (23), the foundations and two or three courses above the ground were built of masonry to protect the oak against damp. On top of this was laid a sill-piece, into which were framed the uprights, called studs; and the earlier the work is, the closer the studs come together. Above the studs was another horizontal sill; and the joists of the floor were rested on this and projected over the framing under. So, stage by stage, the floors jutted out until the gables were reached; and these again were finished off with overhanging "barge boards". Here the old carpenters enjoyed themselves by inventing beautiful pierced patterns, almost lace-like in their richness. The roof was sometimes covered with tiles, thatch, or thin stone slabs. The oak studs were filled between with wattle, rather as a hurdle is made now, and then plastered, and this is called wattle-and-daub work; or brick was used for the same purpose, and this is called brick-nogging. The naked oak was generally allowed to take on a pleasant grey tint by exposure to the weather. The appearance of many half-timbered houses has been ruined in modern times by being tarred; for the result is altogether too startlingly black and white to be agreeable.

24 A Tile-hung House, near Chiddingfold, Surrey

Fig. 24 shows a very pleasant old house near Chiddingfold, Surrey. Here the outer walls on the first floor have been covered with tiles; and architects describe this treatment as tile-hanging. In these days the papers are full of complaints against people who ruin the look of the country by building bungalows. If they would only go to work as the old builders did, we should not have so many complaints. If all the old quarries were opened up, and the local brickyards started again, English country life would benefit. Decay set in before 1914 when bricks produced by large commercial concerns were used to undersell the products of the smaller brickfields. Once the latter had been driven out of business, country brickmakers drifted to the towns seeking for employment. In the end nobody was much better off, because the price of the imported bricks rose, until they were as dear as—or dearer than—the country-made variety.

Fig. 25, of the sixteenth-century barn at Edlesborough, Buckinghamshire, shows a magnificent example of old carpenters' work. It is ten bays in length; each bay is about 16 feet wide, and the width is about 29 feet between the walls. This barn has a cathedral-like dignity. Nowadays, corn is stacked in the fields, and the threshing machine taken to the rick. In the old days it was carted to the barn and stored there, and threshed

25 Sixteenth-century Barn at Church Farm, Edlesborough, Buckinghamshire

by flails on a good oak floor by the open door. A flail is described in our eighteenth-century chapter (136).

Now we turn to the kind of life that would have been lived in the houses we have been describing, and the everyday things that would have been used there. A good deal of information can be obtained from old wills; and we give extracts from one that the authors of this book find particularly interesting. Thomas Quenell, of Lythe Hill, Chiddingfold, yeoman, died in 1571, and this is how he disposed of his possessions:

> ffirste, I geve and bequethe my sowle into the hands of Almightie God my maker and his sonne Jesu Christe my redeamer throughe whose deathe and passion I truste to be saved and to have a gloryous and Joyefull resurrection emonge the nūber of his electe.

There are various charitable bequests, but what especially concerns us here is the description he gives of the various parts of his house and the careful provision he makes for the comfort of his wife Agnys:

> Itm̃, I geve and bequethe to Agnys my wyfe enduringe the tyme of her naturall lyfe my parler in the weste syde of my house at Lythehill w^{c}h adioynethe to the hawle there, the chamber over the same pler, the garret above the same chamber, the lofte over the hawle and the kytchen lofte w^{t}h free ingres, egress and regres. Roome and fyer in the said hawle at all tymes and also halfe the kytchen, and fyer boote [firewood] to dresse meate and drinke, bake and brewe, and to doe all other necessaryes mete and convenyent in the same kytchen at all tymes and halfe the newe coope nowe standinge in the sayde kytchen.

Outside the house itself, Agnys was to have

> all my oulde stable w^{c}h adioynethe to the weste syde of my house, the weste ende of my Raynge [barn or granary] to laye haye or strawe in, and halfe the rest of my Raynge, and also the upper gates for her cattayles, [as well as] all my herber [garden] w^{c}h adioynethe to the easte syde of my saide house. And all my orcharde w^{c}h adioynethe to the sayde herber on the sowethe syde of my sayde house from the newe pale that adioynethe unto the sayde herber on the easte syde unto the home felde on the weste syde and extendethe from the sayde house on the northe syde unto the lyttle meade on the sowethe syde.

The plan (27) will help to explain how the house and its surroundings were arranged.

When Agnys dies, the whole property is to revert to Robert, a brother, the heir, and who is to share the house with Agnys during her lifetime. She has a good deal of land left to her in other places, and a barn is mentioned, but for this she had to pay a rent to Robert. Thomas leaves to "Elynor Qwennell my cossyn twoe eweshipe", and £51 13*s*. 4*d*. to be paid "to her at the daye of her maryage. And I will that she contynue until the tyme of her marriage in service wth Agnys my wife."

Robert Page, a servant, has one cow and £6 14*s*. 4*d*.; Willm Wodier, another servant, "one hecforde [heifer] bullocke; Willm Allyn three ewe teggs; Agnys Todman one hecforde bullocke". Brothers and a brother-in-law are remembered, and "I geve to eũy one of my godchildren xijd. [12*d*.] that will requyre to have the same." Then the will goes back to Agnys, the wife, who is to have

> Sixe of my beste keene (except one cowe named Lustye) fower hecforde wherof one black w^{t}h a whitte sterre in the forhed, one Redde wyth a whitte backe, one other Redde w^{t}h a chynned [narrow strip of white] face and one browne w^{t}h a whitte face.

She was also to receive

> six of my best oxen w^{t}h yokes and chaynes meete for them, my newe wollen wheles, my yonge baye Amblynge mare, my blacke Amblynge mare w^{t}h a whitte steare in the forhed, twoe steares nowe goynge in Anstrode, the one havinge a brended [brindled] face and the other being a vallower steare w^{t}h a whitte face.

Other bequests to Agnys included two other heifers, twelve ewes, twelve lambs, "my fyve hogge of one sorte beinge aboute twoe yeares oulde at Michaelmas laste, twoe Redde hogge goyne emonge my wylde hogges", and half the wheat, rye, and oats growing, and one acre of grass Thomas had bought and which was "to be mowen made and caryed awaye w^{t}hin fortenighte after mydsomer nexte". Thomas left to his wife

> all my poultrey whatsoever my three beste beddes w^{t}h boulsters pyllowes and pyllowe coate belonging to them, my beste bedstedle (excepte one) all my sheate (excepte three payer of canvas sheate),

26 "My Leaste Skyllet"

all my beste blanckete (except one payer), my three best coverlette and one Qwylte, all my pewter vessyll, (except fyve pewter platters twoe pewter disshes and one basone wch were my fathers), my beste and my leaste twoe candlestycke, my beste brasse potts, my beste and my leaste twoe kettles, and my kettle wch was bounde wth yron by Hewghe the Smythe, my posnet [a little pot] of belle brasse, my leaste Skyllet [pot with long handle(26)]of brasse, and the occupacon of my Cawdron as often as she shall have nede, so long tyme as she shall be dwellinge at Lyethehill aforsayde, and also halfe of alman9 of my wodden vessill to be equally divyded (excepte my beste vate and my best kyfe) [tub used in brewing].

Thomas left to his wife

halfe my bakon at the beame (excepte the twoe greateste flytches and the twoe leaste flytches) halfe my Larde and greace, twoe of the beste flytches of dryed beefe, twoe of my beste table clothes, twoe of my beste towels, halfe of all my table napkyns, one dozen of my beste spons, my three beste soup cuppes, the beste cheste wch I nowe have to my selfe, and all the resedue of my cofers (except the beste of them) wch coferys nowe ys in the tenure of my sayd wyfe.

But the residue "of all my goode cattayls and chattayls moveables and unmoveables" went to Robert, Thomas Quenell's brother.

The importance of this will is that it gives us an excellent idea of the house, its surroundings, and what it contained; and one feels the better for knowing the name of that Elizabethan cow "Lustye". Lythe Hill still stands on the road from Haslemere to Anstead Brook; but alterations have made the house not so suitable for illustration as the one we have selected(24).

The plan(27), in conjunction with the sketch of the exterior of the house, will explain the position of the rooms. The hall was as high as the ground and first floors at the two ends: which means that there were separate staircases to the two chambers—probably Robert the heir had the one over the kitchen. The servants would have slept in the garrets, as they had begun to do during the fifteenth century. The plan demonstrated that among the simpler country folk the old medieval type of arrangement

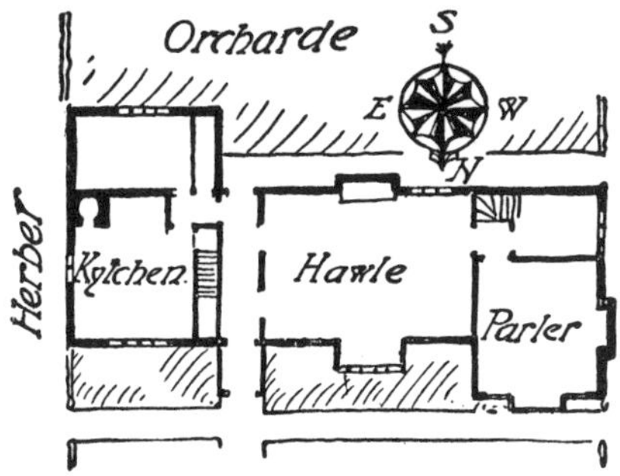

27 Plan of a House

was still adhered to; this can be seen by reference to the houses in Vol. I. At the same time, if the plan had been extended on the left hand by a buttery and winter parlour, it would have developed into the ⊓ type of plan—a form said to have been adopted by way of compliment to Queen Elizabeth. Whole families were used to living together in those days; and it enabled them to have a single fine house instead of many small ones.

> More hath built neare London [Erasmus wrote to a friend], upon the Thames side, a commodious house, neither meane nor subject to envie, yet magnificent enough; there he converseth affably with his family, his wife, his son and daughter-in-lawe, his three daughters and their husbands, with eleven grandchildren.

It is unlikely that the vanished Beaufort House at Chelsea shown in fig. 31 was the one More built; but it is of the style of his period or a little later, and shows the kind of gardens that surrounded the dwellings of the time, and which had altered but little in style when this engraving was made.

Agnys seems to have had the larger share of the house at Lythe Hill; and poor Robert had to be content with the chamber over the kitchen. He added a wing to the house later, dying in 1612, forty-one years after Thomas. Agnys, it is clear, intended to carry on farming operations on her own account. As for Thomas Quenell's servants, they must have had holdings of land, to feed the cattle and stock he left them.

A modern farm labourer would be rather embarrassed by the bequest of a cow or even "one hecforde bullocke".

LAND-HOLDING

To understand Elizabethan country life, and the change that came over England during the sixteenth century, we must consider both how land was held at that time and how (as we have already described) it had been held in the Middle Ages.

First, let us summarise the medieval system. In a typical manor of the Middle Ages, the lord retained perhaps one-third of the land for his own use. This was called the demesne; but it was not enclosed or fenced off, and formed part of the arable land on which crops were grown. The remainder was divided between the villeins, and farmed by them for the common benefit. They shared the hay grown on the meadows; and their pigs, under the charge of the swineherds, fed on the acorns in the woodlands. The villagers paid for their share of the common fields by working for the lord on the demesne land for two or three days in the week; and sometimes they paid a little in kind—eggs, fowls or the like—with the additional obligation of following their lord to war.

This method of farming was called the open-field system, and did not altogether die out in England until the end of the eighteenth century.

The enclosures, of which we hear so much, started with the demesne land, and were due to two main causes—the scarcity of labour after the Black Death of 1348, and the growth of the wool trade, which made it more profitable to keep sheep, and sell wool, than to grow corn. The lord often withdrew his demesne lands in the common fields, and put them down to pasture. This proved helpful at first, because less labour was required to tend sheep than to grow corn; and the waste lands were enclosed for the same purpose. Later on, however, as the population increased, it caused great hardship and threw many labourers out of work. In Vol. I we explained how some of the landowners who could not get men to work their land as villeins, began to let it

28 A Water-carrier

on stock and land leases, charging a rent. From the class thus created the yeomen developed; and, if we can judge by the number of small houses they built in the fifteenth and sixteenth centuries, they must have been a prosperous body. But the sixteenth century saw the emergence of an altogether different spirit. In the Middle Ages land was held to produce food, and to guarantee a supply of sturdy men-at-arms. With the dissolution of the monasteries, nearly one-fifteenth of England changed hands. Whereas, under the old system, the land was worked for the common good, the new method allowed the pushing man to forge ahead, making money as best he might, often at his fellows' expense.

Sir Thomas More's *Utopia* was published in 1516; and this is how he describes the operations of early sixteenth-century land enclosures:

> The husbandmen be thrust oute of their owne, or els either by coveyne and fraude, or by violent oppression they be put besydes it, or by wronges and injuries thei be so weried, that they be compelled to sell all: by one meanes therfore or by other, either by hooke or crooke they must needes departe awaye, poore, selye, wretched soules.

Until the beginning of the sixteenth century, the monks had given alms, assisted sick and needy folk, and entertained travellers. After the suppression of the monasteries, a great many people lost their homes; and this happened at a time when the number of men employed on the farms was being reduced by enclosures and sheep-keeping. To remedy the miserable state of affairs that resulted, the Tudor sovereigns passed numerous laws. Vagabonds were to be whipped and put in the stocks. No one must hold more than one farm, or keep more than 2,000 sheep. Crops must be grown, buildings repaired, and men employed. It was not, however, until the middle of Elizabeth's reign that conditions improved. Then meat and corn began to fetch a better price, while the price of wool declined; and this made the growing of crops and keeping of cattle profitable, and provided more employment. Fitzherbert's book, published in 1523, gave a new impetus to the art of agriculture.

Since we are writing of country life, we include another drawing to illustrate the development of the windmill (29);

29 A Post-mill

though the mill shown, which is still in existence, must not be regarded as typical of the sixteenth century. In Vol. I, Chapter IV, we reproduced an illustration of a post-mill—so called because the whole structure was balanced and turned on a great oak post set up and securely strutted. Here, if the wind changed, the mill had to be turned round on its post by hand, until the main sails came into the wind. And, as this was very hard work, the millwright hit upon an ingenious labour-saving contrivance, shown in fig. 29, which consisted of a vane set up on the end of the long fantail, or steps at the back of the mill. The vane did not operate while the main sails were in the wind; but if it changed and blew from the side, the vane came into action, and its spindle, by means of bevel gears, turned the vertical shafting on the left, which by more gears moved the carriage supporting the fantail around a circular track. Remember, the whole mill above the circular round house turned on its central post; so that, as it was moved by the action of the vane, the main sails would come into the wind, while the vane turned out of it and thus stopped. The iron wheel and chain, hanging from the balcony, operated a spindle through the main shaft, which opened and shut the louvres on the sails. The little balcony is a very agreeable piece of design; and the chute for sacks at the side of the steps should also be noticed.

GREAT HOUSES

From the yeoman's comparatively modest dwelling and the life of an Elizabethan farm, we must now pass on to the neighbouring great house.

Fig. 30 gives the plan of one of the larger houses, such as were built by the more considerable landowners at the end of Queen Elizabeth's reign. *A* shows the ground floor, raised sufficiently

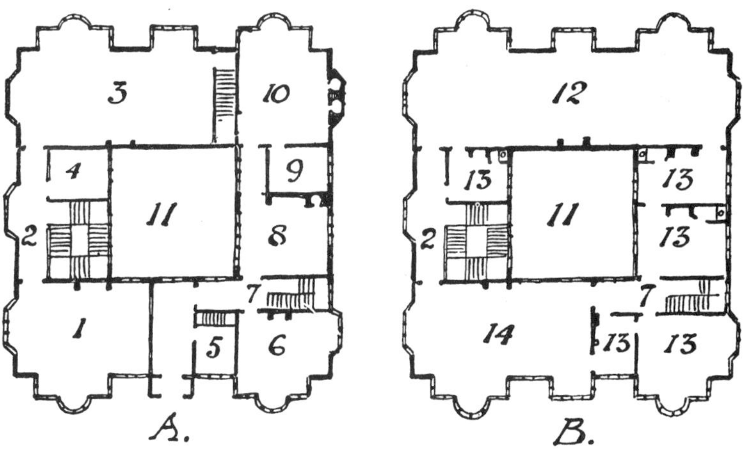

30 Plan of an Elizabethan House

to have cellars beneath. The entrance is by way of the screens, into the hall at 1. The principal staircase is at 2, and the parlour 3 has a smaller room off it at 4. At 5 is the buttery, with the winter parlour at 6, back stairs 7, kitchen 8, pastry 10, with the bolting-house off it at 9, and 11 is the inner court. *B* is the first floor, access to which is gained by the staircases 2 and 7; 12 is the gallery, 14 the great chamber, and 13 the bedrooms. It will be noticed that this type of plan follows in many ways that of the fifteenth-century house shown in Vol. I, Chapter IV. The hall, winter parlour, and kitchen offices occur in much the same position, but the house has better accommodation, and is planned in a more compact style, with the rooms arranged round an inner court, or spread out like an ПП or **H**. The compact courtyard type develops in the next century into a solid block of building, as we shall see later on.

The basement kitchen was a horror imported from Italy—at Barlborough as early as 1583; but it is more characteristic of the seventeenth century. Now, as to the uses of the rooms; the hall still remained the central feature of the plan, and was used for dining, but it was customary for the steward to preside in the hall, and for the family to have their meals in the winter parlour. This, of course, was an improvement in domestic comfort. The pastry was the Elizabethan name for the bakehouse; and the bolting-house was a sort of flour store where it could be bolted or sifted. All this part of the house is very well planned from the practical point of view; meals could be prepared in the kitchen, and put on to the table in the hall, or winter parlour, without being chilled by journeys through long passages, as happened in the next century. Meals were large and very elaborate. Gentry usually dined at eleven, dinner often occupying three hours, and supped about six o'clock. Merchants and farmers dined at noon, and supped at seven or eight. Breakfast was usually taken as an early snack. Meat-eating was excessive; but fish was beginning to come into fashion among the upper classes. Although, according to Thomas Tusser—

> Good ploughman look weekly of Custom and right,
> For roast meat on Sunday, Thursdays at night,

the usual meal partaken in a labourer's cottage probably consisted of bread (with an admixture of rye in it), bacon, milk,

31 Beaufort House, by the Thames at Chelsea, *c*. 1585, now destroyed
From an Engraving by Kip

curds and perhaps beer or cider. Brawn was a favourite dish among all classes—hogs were specially bred to provide it.

The store cupboard in a large home was always well filled, for we must remember that the housewife had to be ready to receive at any time a large influx of visitors; and, in the country at least, there were no shops that she could fall back on. Hence we read of the salting down of barrels of fish, meat, and, in the store cupboard, of pepper, mace, cloves, ginger, figs, raisins, hops, honey, oil, vinegar, salt, almonds, dates, saffron and cinnamon. Pastries and cakes were made and jellies of all colours. Stale ale (or ale a year old) and strong beer, metheglin, cider, and perry were conserved in large quantities, besides fifty-six different sorts of wine.

Roasting was still done on the spit, and baking either in iron boxes placed in the fire, or in the brick oven at the side of the fireplace. No china was as yet used. Among the poor, wooden platters and drinking vessels were gradually being replaced by pewter; while the rich were beginning to use silver, as well as glass from Venice and delft-ware from Holland. A rough English pottery had long been made, "pots of earth of sundry colours and moulds [Harrison tells us] many with pewter rims".

We saw how in the thirteenth, fourteenth, and fifteenth centuries the lord's solar was always placed upstairs. The habit continued in the sixteenth century; and the great chamber at 14 answers to our drawing-room. In a noble's house it would have been called the presence chamber, but it might have included a bed. This was a survival of the time when the solar was parlour, presence chamber, and bedroom all rolled into one. The long gallery at 12 is another typical feature of Elizabethan and Jacobean plans. Often of great length, it must have made a delightful addition to a house, a splendid place for romps and games, or for the display of pictures and fine furniture. There were now many more bedrooms, and good attics for the servants; but passages were still few, and one room often opened into another.

Fig. 32 is of the exterior of the house; and our readers will at once notice that some very considerable change has come over the spirit of design. This house is different from those of the thirteenth, fourteenth, and fifteenth centuries, which were all

32 An Elizabethan House

Drawing founded on the Hall, Bradford-on-Avon

closely related. It shows the beginning of Renaissance design, or rebirth of the old classical forms of architecture.

We have seen how, at the fall of Constantinople in 1453, the scholars who fled from that city spread the knowledge of classical literature and architecture; but Italian designers had not so much to learn from the classical past as architects in northern countries. They were familiar with the ruins of Roman buildings; and Gothic architecture never obtained the same hold, or adopted quite the same forms, among the Italians as it did among the French and English. This becomes clear if one compares such Italian cathedrals as Siena and Orvieto with their northern counterparts.

The Renaissance movement had started earlier in Italy. Filippo Brunelleschi (1377–1446), fired by the classical tradition, was the first of the Italian architects to work in the new manner; and the Pazzi Chapel in Florence was built early in the fifteenth century. Donatello the sculptor, born 1386, died 1466; he was

33 The Tomb of Henry VII

followed by the other giants of the Renaissance, Luca Della Robbia, Botticelli, Leonardo da Vinci, Michelangelo, and Titian, who was born 1477 and died in 1576. Nature was prodigal with genius in the fifteenth century. At length the Renaissance reached the shores of England; and it was the tomb that Henry VIII built for his father in Westminster Abbey that introduced Englishmen to the new style(33). Just as at Westminster, in Henry III's work, we can study Gothic at its finest period, so, in Henry VII's Chapel, we see the culmination in the exquisite fan vaulting of the roof; while the tomb itself illustrates the beginnings of Renaissance art.

Fig. 32 shows that the Elizabethan house was more symmetrical than that of the fifteenth century; the various parts are as exactly balanced as possible. The hall, which, in the previous century, was expressed outside by a separate roof, now forms part of the house and cannot be distinguished from the remainder of the building. The four-centred arches have gone; and the only one that appears is semicircular in shape. The windows have square heads, with label moulds typical of earlier times, and, like the gables, are still Gothic in character. There was so much more window in these times than formerly that we can understand a complaint in one of Lord Bacon's essays: "You shall have sometimes fair houses so full of glass, that one cannot tell where to be come, to be out of the sun or cold." It was said of a famous Derbyshire house, "Hardwick Hall, more glass than wall".

The Elizabethans created an architecture that was amazingly picturesque and fashioned out of the Gothic tradition and what they could pick up of the new Italian fashion. The work was full of vigour. Later on, as the designers came to know more, the work they produced was less lively.

Another interesting development in the sixteenth century was the wooden staircase. Right through the Middle Ages people had been satisfied with circular stone staircases like those in church towers. Sometimes the same form was used in oak, the solid treads being tenoned into a centre newel. Then quite suddenly, in the sixteenth century, beautiful staircases like the one illustrated in fig. 34 began to be made; and henceforward we shall find infinite variety of design and beautiful workmanship used in this part of the house. The same name of newel is given

34 A Sixteenth-century Staircase
Founded on Staircase at the Charterhouse, London

to the square terminal posts; into which were framed the strings, supporting the ends of the treads and risers to the stairs. The hand-rail, again, is framed into the newels; and between string and hand-rail comes the balustrade, formed either with separate balusters, or the beautiful arcaded treatment shown in our sketch.

The Elizabethan builders loved beautiful woodwork, and could command the services of splendid craftsmen. The fifteenth century had been the great period for church woodwork, and many of the most beautiful screens, choir-stalls and pulpits were then made. This work had helped to produce a school of skilful and experienced "joyners", who, in the sixteenth century, seized on the rich possibilities offered by Renaissance ornament. The results they achieved were often astonishingly fine. Fig. 35 illustrates an Elizabethan parlour, and shows walls panelled with oak, and a modelled plaster ceiling. The internal porch to the room is a characteristic and attractive feature, which must have added to its comfort. The elaboration of these interiors may be seen in the plates of Nash's *Mansions*, and in some of the rooms now set up in the Victoria and Albert Museum, such as that from Sizergh, Westmorland, where the panelling is inlaid. There is another fine room at Chastleton, Oxfordshire. The plaster frieze was often painted in gay colours, as at Boughton Malherbe rectory, Kent; and sometimes the windows were filled with fine heraldic stained-glass, as at Ockwells, Berkshire, and the great parlour at Gilling Castle, Yorkshire, perhaps the most splendid interior of all.

The furniture was substantial, but still scarce; and from a writer of 1585 we learn that

> The Royal treasures in furniture and tapestries are kept only in that palace, in which for the time being the Queen resides, and when she moves to another, everything is taken away, only the bare walls are left standing.

FURNITURE

Presses date from early days. These were wardrobes, hanging or shelved, in which clothes were kept. Cupboards, formerly cup-boards (shelves or boards on which were kept the drinking vessels), were by now enclosed and became the livery cupboard, containing the wages in kind or "livery" of the servants, bread,

35 An Elizabethan Parlour

Drawing founded on a Room at Bradninch Manor, Devon

butter, cheese, candles, etc., and the court cupboard, containing dry goods belonging to the master or mistress.

36 A Tudor Chair

Sideboards came into fashion during the Elizabethan period, solely for the display of plate. Nests of oak boxes were sometimes placed in the cupboards and chests as a means of storing goods tidily; but it was not until the seventeenth century that the boxes were placed on runners and developed into the modern chest of drawers. Chairs were still few; and in an inventory of a house with thirty rooms only nineteen chairs are listed. Stools and chests took their place as seats. Opinions differ as to the date of upholstery; but as a rule, except for the ceremonial X-type, chairs were usually provided with loose cushions only.

Tables, of trestle shape in the Middle Ages, were now framed, though still generally heavy and cumbersome. Mirrors of glass, save for a few rare Venetian examples, were unknown. Henry VIII used toilet mirrors of burnished metal and crystal.

No English pile carpet has been found earlier in date than 1570; but many beautiful Oriental specimens were brought into the country. Englishwomen worked carpets in tapestry, embroidery and petit-point. These "carpets" were usually hung on the walls and draped over tables; and rushes, either loose or plaited into a flat covering, were generally laid on the floors.

According to our present ideas, this Tudor habit had little to recommend it, and many obvious disadvantages. If, as is possible, the rushes were allowed to accumulate, they must have been ideal breeding-grounds for insects—a belief confirmed by Tusser's artless but apposite advice:

> While wormwood hath seed, get a bundle or twain
> To save against March, to make flea to refrain
> Where Chamber is swept and that wormwood is strown
> No flea for his life dare abide to be known.

Tusser implies that the floors were regularly swept; but Erasmus, reporting on English life, suggests that the decaying heaps of rushes became a repository of all sorts of filth, and remained uncleared for twenty years, with results decidedly detrimental to health. But possibly the great scholar was exceptionally unfortunate in his experiences; and his chronic ill-health may have made him peevish and inclined to exaggerate. He writes, however, with great appreciation of the charm of the English girls, and their delightful way of kissing the guest when he arrived and departed.

Another Dutch visitor, a medical man called Levine Lemnie, paints, about half a century later, a very much brighter and more attractive picture:

> The neat cleanliness [he remarks], the exquisite finenesse, the pleasaunte and delightful furniture in every poynte for household, wonderfully rejoysed me; their chambers and parlours strawed over with sweete herbs refreshed me; their nosegayes finely intermingled with sundry sorte of fragraunte floures in their bedchambers and privy rooms, with comfortable smell cheered me up and entirely delighted all my senses
>
> (*The Touchstone of Complexion*, 1576).

Contemporary writers have much to say of England's increasing wealth and luxury. One writer notes three improvements: the multitude of "chimneys" (fireplaces) lately erected, feather beds instead of straw pallets, and vessels of wood now giving place to pewter.

> Even many farmers [he adds] also have learned to garnish their cupboards with plate, their joined beds with tapestry and silk hangings, and their tables with carpets [worked tablecloths] and fine napery, whereby the wealth of country doth appear.

William Harrison, however, had his doubts as to the improvements made.

> In times past [he writes], men were contented to dwell in houses built of sallow, willow, plumtree, hardbeam and elm, so that the use of oak was in manner dedicated wholly unto churches, religious houses, prince's palaces, noblemen's lodgings, and navigation; but now all these are rejected, and nothing but oak any whit regarded. And yet see the change! For when our houses were built of willow, then had we oaken men; but now that our houses are come to be made of oak, our men are not only become willow, but a great many, through Persian delicacy crept in among us, altogether of

37 A Sixteenth-century Bed

straw: which is a sore alteration. In those the courage of the owner was a sufficient defence to keep the house in safety, but now the assurance of the timber, double locks and bolts, must defend the man from robbing. Now have we many chimneys [fireplaces]; and yet our tenderlings complain of rheums, catarrhs, and poses. Then had we none but reredosses [movable backs to the fires] and our heads did never ache. For as the smoke in those days was supposed to be a sufficient hardening for the timbers of the house, so it was reported a far better medicine to keep the good man and

38 An Elizabethan Hall, Sixteenth Century
Founded on the Middle Temple Hall, London

his family from the quake or pose, wherewith as then very few were oft acquainted.

Fig. 37 shows an Elizabethan bed; and here again we observe a riot of carving that leaves hardly a square inch of wood unfretted; yet the result is very beautiful. It is amusingly classic;

and the bedposts are turned into very free translations of one of the orders, this time the Ionic. The bedspread, curtains, and valance to the tester would all have been embroidered by hand. We noted, when describing the plan of the bedrooms, how often they were passage rooms, one leading through to another. This was doubtless one of the reasons for the four posts and curtains, and the large size of the beds. One could draw the curtains, and make the bed into the bedroom. Beds were treasured possessions; in the old will we have drawn on, we saw how beds were left as legacies to friends and relations.

Fig. 38 is based on the Hall of the Middle Temple in London, which dates from 1570. It was badly damaged in the Second World War, and the very elaborately carved entrance screen smashed; but it has escaped complete destruction. The roof is a very splendid example of double hammer-beam design, and marks the final development of that type. We saw, in the fifteenth century, how this method of construction was arrived at. In Vol. I we described the various parts of the roof. Here the principal rafters are not visible but occur at each bay, of which the hammer-beams, two on either side, come under principals and are supported by curved braces. Above these comes a collar-beam with an arched brace under it. The purlins are framed in between the principals; and under these again are arched braces which go from hammer-beam to hammer-beam. Now the details and mouldings of this roof are Renaissance in character; but its form is Gothic; and after this period the timbered roof disappears, with its play of light and shade, and its suggestion of mystery and gloom; and we find either flat ceilings or plaster vaults. The windows, too, retain a little of the Gothic character. The screen at the end is a splendid specimen of Elizabethan woodwork, with woodwork a century later round the openings.

GARDENS AND GARDENING

The Tudors were great gardeners and fond of flowers, and their houses were set about with herbers and pleasant courts. There was a fore-court in front, and a base-court, around which were grouped the stables and offices. A terrace against the house overlooked the gardens and parterre. The flower-beds were edged with rosemary, lavender, marjoram and thyme. Fig. 39

shows a delightful little garden that still exists at Hampton Court, and dates from the reign of Henry VIII. Here the King may have walked with Anne Boleyn and the ladies of her Court. This type is called a formal garden; and the design had probably been handed down from medieval times. During the early days, people had to wall in their houses, castles, and monasteries for security; and, even when fortifications were no longer needed, there was still a feeling that any garth, or garden, should have a wall, or hedge, as a frame. This produced a certain air of formality; paths were straight, yews were cut into quaint shapes, called topiary work, and mazes and labyrinths were popular. Such gardens helped to clothe a house and soften the hardness of its structural outline. Gardens and gardening became a vital part of Tudor existence; and, now travel had become safer and easier, many new and interesting plants and trees were brought home from abroad. Red and black currants were introduced from Europe, and so called because they were supposed to be small grapes; though really they are of the gooseberry family. Thomas Cromwell planted rhubarb for medicinal purposes; and apricots, oranges and other hot-weather fruits were now well known. William Harrison had three hundred varieties of simples in his garden; and the great herbalist Gerard had a physic garden in Holborn that included upward of a thousand different kinds of plants.

Here is a contemporary description of a Tudor garden:

> It is so encompassed with parks full of deer, delicious gardens, groves ornamented with trellis work, cabinets of verdure, and walks, that it seems to be a place pitched upon by pleasure herself to dwell in along with health. In the pleasure and artificial gardens are many columns and pyramids of marble, two fountains that spout water, one round, the other like a pyramid upon which are perched small birds that stream water out of their bills. There is, besides, another pyramid of marble full of concealed pipes, which spirt upon all who come within their reach.

These hydraulic jokes appealed to the Tudors, as much as the gardens of which they formed a part.

MUSIC

Now it is time to consider how life was enjoyed in the larger Elizabethan houses. Through the ages, people have amused

39 A Tudor Garden, at Hampton Court

themselves by playing on musical instruments. Before the beginning of history, some cheerful old savage, aiming a blow at a friend, may have hit an old hollow log, and noticed that it gave out a pleasant note. Interested, he repeated the performance, and found that blows of varying strength, on different materials, gave him a range of several notes. Or perhaps he listened to the woodpecker. To some such occasion one might possibly trace back the development of the harmonica, with its graded wood or metal bars, and all the diversity of instruments —drums, gongs, cymbals, triangles, and tambourines—that produce pleasant noises rather than tuneful notes. Or the early musician, sewing up a skin with the intestines of an animal, may have discovered that they were tuneful when dry and stretched, or have noticed that the twang of his bowstring was musical, thus helping to originate harp, monochord, viol, psaltery, dulcimer, spinet, and piano. The origin of the wind instruments is easily guessed: the horns of animals must have provided the inspiration for pipes and flutes, bugles and trumpets, and the noble organ. When Joshua besieged Jericho, he was commanded that "seven priests shall bear before the ark seven trumpets of rams' horns".

40 Henry VIII Playing a Harp

Fig. 40 depicts Henry VIII playing a harp; and the harp has been chosen because it can be accepted as the forerunner of the modern piano. When children of today play on the piano, by means of a very complicated bit of machinery they strike the strings with little hammers, instead of plucking them with their fingers. In musical instruments, as in everything else, men have sought the aid of mechanical devices.

It may be helpful if we give a description of some of the musical instruments our ancestors knew, and show their connection with those in use today. The monochord came into fashion as early as the twelfth century. It had only one string, with a movable bridge, and was generally plucked by the finger although musicians sometimes employed a bow. The organistrum, or symphony, was a development of the monochord. A resined wheel was placed under the string, and turned by a handle at one end. It was also called the *vielle à roue*, or viol with a wheel, or vielle. Little stops at the side were either turned, pulled out, or pressed in, to stop off the strings, just as one does with a violin; and the resined wheel was the mechanical equivalent of the resined bow. The modern hurdy-gurdy is the lineal descendant of the organistrum. It was an aristocratic instrument in the eighteenth century, but the sound it produced must, as the name suggests, always have been rather dismal.

The manichord of the thirteenth century was the first stringed instrument to be played from a keyboard. The clavichord appeared at the end of the fourteenth century, and did not reach its highest development until the beginning of the eighteenth century. It had a very simple keyboard; the finger struck one end of a balanced lever, at the other end of which was a brass pin called a tangent. This not only struck the string but stopped off the length that determined the note; and two or three notes were made on the same string, by different tangents striking at different lengths. Later, each note had its separate string, so it resembled an elementary piano; for the strings were struck by hammers (invented in 1709 by a Florentine) whereas, in the spinet or harpsichord, they were plucked by a metal point, leather spine, or quill, on what is called a jack. The clavicymbal, virginal, and clavecin were all played in this way.

Fig. 41 shows a clavicytherium, or upright spinet of the sixteenth century. Its likeness to a harp is at once apparent. The fingers strike on to a balanced lever, which, by an ingenious contrivance, pushes a jack, with a leather spine on it, through the backboard, and plucks the string. Its compass was about the same as the human voice. We shall see later how the next

41 A Clavicytherium

development was to put the clavicytherium flat on its back; after which the keyboard was rearranged and it was called the spinet, or harpsichord.

The dulcimer, another forerunner of the piano, consisted of a sounding-board across which strings of varying length were stretched, and struck by hammers. Pepys went to a puppet play in Covent Garden, on May 14th, 1662, and recorded in his diary: "Here, among the fiddles, I first saw a dulcimer played on with sticks, knocking of the strings, and is very pretty." The psaltery had the same form as the dulcimer, but was played by plucking the strings.

Many other musical instruments are named by old writers. The viol was like a violin, but with a flat back and pieces of gut across the finger-board, which was played with a bow. Viola-da-gamba was played while held between the knees. "He plays o' the viol-de-gamboys", says Sir Toby Belch of Sir Andrew Aguecheek. The lute was the forerunner of the mandolin, and had a pear-shaped body; the treble lute had a bent head; archlutes were particularly large instruments. The theorbo was lute-shaped and large; the cittern, lute-shaped and small. The gittern was a lute with a fiddle-shaped body; the guitar, one with a flat back. All these instruments were plucked with a plectrum. The rebec was a three-stringed fiddle.

Of the wind instruments the organ is, of course, the most

wonderful, and has ages of history behind it. In medieval times we read of the organ portative—a small pipe organ, carried by a strap over the shoulder, and played with the right hand, while the left worked the bellows. The positive organ was designed for a stationary position. The regal was a sort of harmonium, with bellows behind the keyboard like large flat books. The clarion was a trumpet; the shawm and pomme were double beating reed instruments with bell-shaped ends. The hautboy was the successor to the shawm. Recorders were whistle flutes; the hornpipe had a horn added to the end of a pipe. Cromhorns were like whistle flutes with ends on a curved line. The humble penny whistle is a close relation of the stately organ, which, in fact, is a collection of whistles, played by mechanical means.

In fig. 42 we see a concert being given by nine performers on seven different instruments. Three people not playing are unlikely to be vocalists, for full orchestral pieces were usually quite separate from singing numbers.

The Elizabethans were an intensely musical race; and modern England has a long tradition of song. Today that tradition is

42 An Orchestral Concert, with Virginal, Viol, Viola-da-Gamba, Recorders, Flute, Trombones and Lute

From an Engraving by J. Nel, 1589

43 A Madrigal by William Byrde (1543–1623)

being revived; Englishmen are rediscovering the joy of music; and we have therefore included in this edition a typical song for each century. Fig. 43 gives the music and words of a madrigal by William Byrde (1543–1623). In Thomas Morley's *Plaine and Easie Introduction to Practicale Musicke, set downe in the Form of a Dialogue* (1597), a musical party is described; and we read how

> supper being ended, and musicke bookes (according to the custom) being brought to table, the mistresse of the house presented me with a part, earnestly requesting me to sing; but when,

after many excuses, I protested unfainedly that I could not, every one began to wonder! Yes, some whispered to others, demanding how I was brought up; so that upon shame of mine ignorance, I goe now to seek out mine old friend Master Gnorimus to make myself his scholler.

WEAPONS AND THE ART OF WAR

Now we must take a giant stride from the musical to the military arts. Probably every village and township had butts, for shooting with the bow(44); and the name survives in many modern place-names, such as Newington Butts, in South London. These must have been pleasant places to go to on a sunny afternoon, and watch the archers at practice.

Strutt gives it as his opinion that the cross-bow was introduced "not long before the commencement of the thirteenth century". But it had two serious disadvantages: on a wet day the strings became useless—it could not be protected so easily as the long-bow, for which the archer had a canvas case—and it took longer to get ready for use. The cross-bow, like the early musket, seems to have been mainly used for sea fights and land sieges, where there was better cover, and less risk of the

44 Archery Butts

long-bowman turning the cross-bowman into an imitation of a feathered porcupine while he was preparing his weapon.

In the regulations for use of the cross-bow, we find the following sentence:

> In case any person should be wounded, or slain in these sports, with an arrow shot by one or another of the archers, he that shot the arrow was not to be sued or molested, if he had, immediately before the discharge of the weapon, cried out "Fast!" the signal usually given upon such occasions.

The Anglo-Saxons, Danes, and the Normans used the long-bow; and at Crécy and Agincourt it was the chief weapon. Afterwards Henry V used gunpowder and guns, and the bow was forgotten, or regarded as obsolete, although the first guns and muskets were cumbersome and feeble devices.

The long-bow lasted well on into the seventeenth century; and, as late as the reign of Charles I, commissions were appointed to survey land adjoining London, and restore it where it had been encroached upon, so that archers might have space to practise. The finest bows were made of yew; and, in Edward IV's time, the height of the bow was the same as that of the archer. The bowstring was of hemp, flax, or silk. The arrow used at Agincourt was a yard long. The shaft, or wand, was made of ash, oak, or birch, and was feathered from the wing of a grey goose. The archer had a bracer, or close sleeve, laced on the left arm, so that the sleeve did not get in the way of the bow-string. A sixteenth-century writer gives instructions on how to stand when shooting, how to hold the bow and draw the bow-string. The archer is warned to watch the mark, not the arrow end. During the Elizabethan Age, even though archery was beginning to be more of a sport than a warlike pursuit, English archers had not forgotten their skill; and, in their heyday, we are told, the shafts they sped "could pierce any armour".

From an old ballad about Robin Hood we learn that at a trial of archery before the king, "he clave the wand in two" from a distance of 400 yards. Cloudesle anticipates William Tell's feat. An apple is placed on his son's head at 120 yards distance.

> And then drew out a fayre brode arrowe;
>   Hys bow was great and longe,
> He set that arrowe in his bowe
>   That was both styffe and stronge.

Then Cloudesle cleft the apple in two,
  As many a man myght se;
Over Gods forbode [God forbid], sayde the kynge
  That thou sholde shute at me.

An Act passed by Henry VIII ordered that no one who had reached the age of twenty-four years should shoot at any mark at less than 220 yards distance. So perhaps the 400 yards range attributed to Robin Hood was not an exaggeration.

> Every village [we are informed] in time of war was expected to provide an archer, a gunman, a pikeman and a billman at the very least, as well as a store of corselets, almaines, rivets, shirts of mail and jacks quilted and covered with leather, fustian or canvas over thick plates of iron that are sewed in the same.

It is interesting to watch the gradual development of the gun, which was destined to supersede the bow. It developed from the cannon; and the earliest type of cannon was made of iron bars, forged together and bound with hoops, the whole being mounted on a stout plank. Stone cannon-balls were often used; hence the name sometimes used, peterara. Gunpowder seems to have developed from the Greek fire of medieval times. The early gun resembled a small cannon mounted on a stick, and fired by hand with a match, like the wick in a cigarette-lighter of today. This type, used in the Wars of the Roses, was called a culverin.

The matchlock, arquebus, or serpentine was invented at

45 A Halberdier, 1572

the beginning of the sixteenth century. It continued in use until the seventeenth century; and the gunner used a rest, which the man in fig. 46 holds in his left hand. The early arquebusier could fire only ten to twelve shots in an hour, and at the end of Elizabeth's reign not more than thirty to forty. Wet weather spoiled the powder; wind and rain put out the match; and for a long time the bowmen laughed at it, and bow and musket were used side by side.

The first step towards the organisation of dragoon regiments was taken at the Battle of Pinkie in 1547, when arquebusiers were mounted. In the "Ballad of Brave Lord Willoughby", composed about 1588, we read this exhortation:

"Stand to it, noble pikemen,
And look you round about!
And shoot you right, you bowmen,
And we will keep them out;

You musket and calliver men
Do you prove true to me,
And I'll be foremost in the fight,"
Says brave Lord Willoughby.

46 A Musketeer, 1550

It was Henry VIII who began to organise a regular army. Each county was governed by a Lord-Lieutenant; and it was his duty to appoint officers and procure a certain number of fighting men from each parish. All men belonging to the same band, or levy, were put into the uniform settled by their shire; and the only feature common to all these uniforms was St. George's cross in red on each man's jerkin.

The cannon used towards the end of the century were far heavier and made more effective weapons than the primitive ordnance shown in illuminations of about 1500. Fig. 48 gives a graphic impression of the storming of a city, with high walls which have been considerably battered by

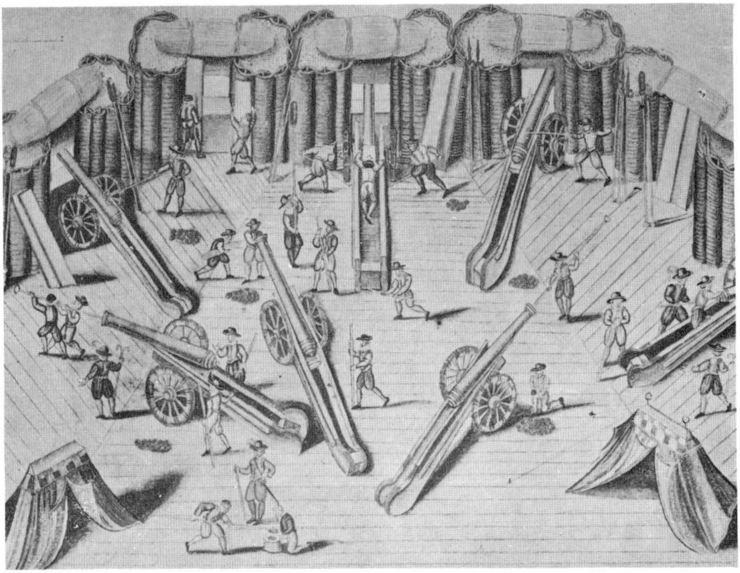

47 A Siege Battery in Active Operation
From a Contemporary Drawing

48 Bombardment and Siege Attack of a Walled City
From a Contemporary Woodcut in Holinshed's "Chronicles"

the cannonade, while the defenders reply with guns mounted in turrets. Fig. 47 is from a careful contemporary drawing of the inside of a well-arranged siege battery, in active operation behind its protecting rampart of fascines.

OUTDOOR SPORTS

Next we come to Elizabethan sports; and here every reader who is at home in the hunting field should consult Turberville's *Booke of Hunting*, published in 1576, and reprinted by the Clarendon Press in 1908. It deals with

> The Noble Arte of Venerie or Hunting—Wherein is handled and set out the Vertues, Nature, and Properties of siuetene sundrie Chaces togither, with the order and maner how to Hunte and kill eueryone of them.

So, at the end of the sixteenth century, Turberville does for hunting what Edward, Duke of York, did at the beginning of the fifteenth; and he, like the "Master of Game", must have been a delightful fellow, and his book is "great joy and liking" to the hunter of today. Among "houndes" Turberville mentions fallow, "dunne, blacke houndes auncientiy come from Sainct Hubert's abbay in Ardene" as sixteenth-century breeds. The "best bringing up of whelpes" is discussed; "How a Kennell ought to be situate and trimmed for Houndes"; and their training is carefully described. Turberville also devotes chapters to the "Nature and Subtilties of Hartes", and "How the Huntsman should go to seeke an Harte in small groues or hewts, beyng priuily enclosed within the greater springs in the Forests and strong couerts."

Fig. 49 shows a sixteenth-century meet, or "the place where and howe an assembly should be made, in the presence of a Prince, or some honorable person". Here Turberville breaks into rhyme:

> The place should first be pight, on pleasant gladsome greene,
> Yet under shade of stately trees, where little sunne is seene;
> And neare some fountaine spring, whose crystall running streames,
> May helpe to coole the parching heate, ycaught by Phœbus' beames.

Then we are told that, "such a place once founde, the Butler first appeares", and he certainly appears to some purpose; for

49 The Assembly Before the Hunt

we are given details of the food provided at this substantial hunt breakfast; and again Turberville goes off into verse:

For whiles colde kynes of Veale, colde Capon, Beefe and Goose,
With Pygeon pyes, and Mutton colde, are set on hunger loose,
And make the forelorne hope, in doubt to scape full hard.
Then come to giue a charge in flanke (else all the marte were marde),
First Neates' tongs poudred well, and Gambones of the Hogge,
Then Saulsages and sauery knackes, to set men's myndes on gogge.

Turberville does not tell us whether this banquet was followed by a little nap. But meanwhile the harbouring of the deer and the setting of relays had taken place. Describing "How to set Relayes", he explains that

> . . . it is requisite to set men abroad which are brought up in hunting, and understande well their aduauntages, and with them a good pricker or huntsman on horsebacke, mounted upon a good curtall, which should be lightly clad, hauing good bootes and high, with an horne about his necke.

At daybreak they have to set out for the place appointed for their relay, and leave their hounds coupled there at the foot of a tree. They then set out to see if they can "discouer the Hart". This done, the huntsman must lead his hounds coupled or

> tyed unto the tracke, and let them folow so three or foure paces right, then let him cast of one, and if he take it right, then may he uncouple the rest, and blowe to them.

"Then he which seemed to have harbored the greatest and oldest Deare", reports to "the Prince or Lorde", who by this time has recovered from the hunt breakfast, and takes his "bloodhounde", with all the prickers or hunters on horseback, every one with a good cudgel in his hand "called a Hunting coodgell or a Troncheon to turne the boughes and beare them from his face as he followeth the houndes in the woodes or thickes". The huntsman, who has harboured the quarry, then goes "before them and rowze the Deare, . . . and then the rest cast off their houndes, and he and all of them crying, 'To him, to him, that's he, that's he!' and such other words of encouragement". The bloodhound was used at a check "untill they haue rowzed or founde him againe with their bloudhounde". Hounds

50 "To flye at the Hearon, according to Martine"
From Turberville's "The Booke of Falconrie" (1575)

were encouraged by name, thus: "Hyke a Bewmont, Hyke Hyke, to him, to him!" A great deal of interesting advice is given on how to overcome the many stratagems employed by the hart to escape pursuit. Chapter XLI deals with "Howe to kill an Hart when he is at bay, and what is then to be doone." If the hart is in deep water, the huntsman is to couple up his hounds, and "stand close and upon a cleare winde, he may chance to haue a blowe at him with his sworde as he [the hart] commeth out"; or a boat is to be obtained, or if the huntsman can swim, he is to do so, dagger in hand, avoiding the "swrede blowe" the hart may give him.

"The breaking up of the Deare", chosen as the subject of our frontispiece, is thus described by Turberville. The Prince or cheif dismounts

> and takes assaye of the Deare with a sharpe knyfe, the whiche is done in this maner. The deare being layd upon his backe, the Prince, chiefe, or such as they shall appoint, commes to it: And the chiefe huntsman (kneeling, if it be to a Prince) doth holde the Deare by the forefoote, whiles the Prince or chief, cut a slyt drawn alongst the brysket of the deare, somewhat lower than the brysket towards the belly. This is done to see the goodness of the flesh, and howe thicke it is.

51 Falconry

From Turberville's "The Booke of Falconrie" (1575)

Then "we use to cut off the Deares' heades. And that is commonly done also by the chiefe personage". Various other portions of the hart are broken up and the hounds rewarded.

Turberville adds a criticism of the huntsmen he knew; and the cap fits as well today as it did in the sixteenth century:

> But nowe adayes I see fewe hunt the Harte as he ought to be hunted; for men give not their hounds leysure to hunt, neither is there passing two or three that can hunt: for there are so many hunters on horsebacke which can neither blow, hallow, nor prick perfectly, which mingle themselues amongst the hounds, crossing them, and breaking their course, in such sort, that it is not possible they should hunt truly: and therefore I say, that it is the horses which hunt, and not the hounds.

So there were thrusters even in those days.

Turberville had already published *The Booke of Falconrie* in 1575; and we have reproduced two of the illustrations from this volume in figs. 50 and 51. He discusses the technique of hawking as thoroughly as the "Noble Arte" of hunting. The drawings are excellent, with splendid details of contemporary costume. The left-hand figure in fig. 51 is wearing padded trunks which reach to the knees, while his retainers still keep to short trunks and trunk hose.

THE STAGE

From country sports we pass on to town amusements; and here we must bear in mind the growing importance of the Elizabethan theatre.

The old Morality Plays, to which we referred in Vol. I, were still performed in the sixteenth century; but gradually, as the Renaissance opened up new horizons, and men became interested in classical literature, a new school of dramatists arose; until, at the end of the century, Shakespeare's genius was to make this period of the art for ever memorable. The publication of Spenser's *Faerie Queene*, about 1589, came as a revelation. The literary men of the early sixteenth century still thought of Latin as the only tongue for educated persons; and, besides being the greatest poem written since Chaucer's *Canterbury Tales*, Spenser's allegory provided a vivid illustration of the poetic possibilities of our own language.

There were many dramatists before Shakespeare; and the

first group that sprang into prominence included Marlowe, Peele, Greene, and Nash. They worked between 1580 and 1590, and introduced plays that were a picturesque jumble of good and bad—a reflection of their adventurous bohemian lives. The Elizabethans had many shortcomings; but dullness was not among their faults. They took ordinary words, and made them sparkle with laughter, or filled them full of tragic meaning.

Shakespeare started his theatrical life about 1585, and appears to have made free use of his predecessors' work. Greene, when dying, seems to have complained of this habit; for he writes of " . . . an upstart crow, beautified with our feathers . . . the only Shake-scene in a country". Chapman and Marston were companions of Shakespeare. Now, just as very little is known of Shakespeare himself, not a great deal is known of the Elizabethan theatre. Fig. 52 has been made from an original sketch of the "Swan" Theatre, by Johannes de Witt, who visited London about 1600. The "Swan" was built at Bankside, in Southwark, on the south side of the Thames—then, as now, a rather grubby place. Its grubbiness, however, did not worry the sixteenth-century playgoer, who went in a delightful way, by boat, the most usual method in those days of getting about London. There was also the "Rose" (1592), Shakespeare's "Globe", and the "Theatre" in Shoreditch. Plays were often given in the galleried yards of inns; and we shall see later how this influenced the design of the theatres.

Another source of information on the Elizabethan theatre is a contract, dated "the eighte daie of Januarye 1599", between "Phillipp Henslowe and Edwarde Allen—on th' one parte, and Peeter Streete, cittizein and carpenter—on th' other parte". Peeter agreed for £440 to build a "newe howse and stadge for a plaie-howse", Edward Alleyn, as the name is now spelled, in 1619 founded Dulwich College, where the contract is preserved; and, like Shakespeare, he appears to have made money, and led a sober life, very different from the bohemian poets who had preceded him. Henslowe managed a company of players at the "Rose", of which Shakespeare was a member in 1592.

The theatre that Peeter built was called the "Fortune", situated "nere Goldinge Lane in the parishe of Sainte Giles withoute Cripplegate". It was remarkable in that it was square, while most of the others were circular. It was "to conteine fowerscore foote of lawfull assize everye waie within". This gives us some idea of the size of the plan of the "Fortune". So far as height was concerned, the contract stipulated for

> the said frame to conteine three stories in heighth, the first or lower storie to conteine twelve foote of lawfull assize in heighte, the seconde storie eleaven foote, . . . and the third or upper storie . . . nyne foote. All which stories shall conteine twelve foote and a half of lawfull assize in breadth throughoute, besides a juttey forwardes in eyther of the saide twoe upper stories of tenne ynches

52 An Elizabethan "Plaie" House

> of lawfull assize; with fower convenient divisions for gentlemen's roomes, and other sufficient and convenient divisions for twoe-pennie rooms.

The "Fortune" was to be fitted up inside

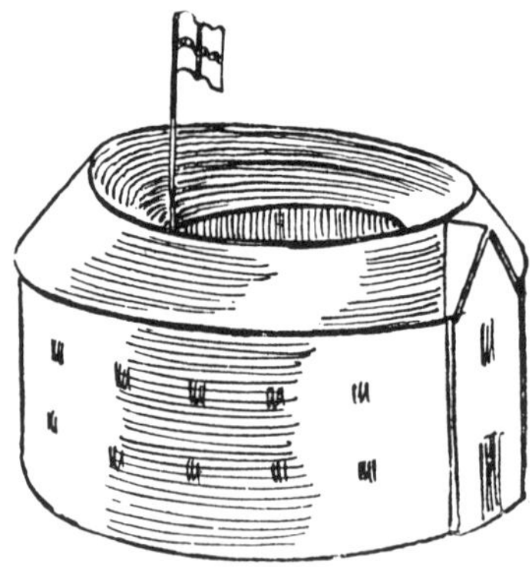

53 The "Globe" Theatre

> with suche like steares, conveyances, and divisions, withoute and within, as are made and contryved in and to the late erected plaie-howse on the Banck, in the saide parishe of Saint Saviours, called the Globe; with a stadge and tyreinge-howse to be made, erected and sett up within the saide frame; with a shadowe or cover over the saide stadge.

Now, excepting only that the "Fortune" was square in plan, this contract very clearly agrees with the details of the "Swan" shown in Johannes de Witt's sketch, from which we have made our drawing. The "Globe" was octagonal in plan until it was burnt down in 1613, when it appears to have been rebuilt on circular lines like the "Swan". Fig. 53 has been made from a print by Hollar of 1647 which shows its later form. Close by, on the same print, we see another circular building called the "Beere baytine Hall" (54), which shows how very similar the two sorts of buildings were. Lambard's *Perambulation of Kent*, 1576, confirms this point:

> Those who go to Paris Garden [where the "Swan" was], the "Bell Savage" [an inn in Ludgate Hill], and the "Theatre" [in Shoreditch] to behold bear-baiting, interludes, or fence play, must not account of any pleasant spectacle unless first they pay one penny at the gate, a second at the entry of the scaffold [or stage], and a third for quiet sitting.

So that apparently the theatres, if necessary, were also for bear-baiting and wild beast shows. In the "Fortune" contract it is specified that the lower storey be "fenced off with strong yron

54 "Beere Baytine Hall"

pykes", which suggests that the wild beasts were to be kept safely in the pit. Both theatre and bear-baiting hall were built on much the same sort of plan, and undoubtedly founded on the ancient arenas where the spectators sat round and watched the spectacle, the galleries evidently being added after the fashion of the old inns like the "Bell Savage".

Lambard tells us that you paid to go into the pit, and then made additional payments for entry into other parts of the house. The pit was open to the sky; and this, combined with the dangerous state of the streets after dark and the difficulties of lighting, led to the performances being given in daylight. On a sunny day, with a blue sky and the gay colours of people's dresses, the sight must indeed have been a pretty one. The stage, as shown, was set up on a scaffold, and projected well into the yard or pit. It was open at the sides behind the columns, so that playgoers in the boxes there got a good view of what was going on. It is doubtful whether the two doors at the back of the stage formed part of the structure, or were enclosed by a movable piece of scenery, behind which was an inner stage, used to represent a cavern, or inner room, if the action of the drama called for it. The boxes over were certainly occupied by the players if they needed a balcony or gallery. On the left-hand side of the stage are three gallants. Fashionable young men often sat or stood upon the stage itself.

The scenery is thought to have been sketchy; and, that there might be no mistake, its purpose was sometimes indicated by labels. Women did not act, and their parts were taken by boys. In the turret perched a trumpeter, who tuned up when the play was about to begin. There is a moral in all this: if the Elizabethans were satisfied with an inn yard or bear-baiting hall as a background for their plays, boys and girls of today, with a little ingenuity and enthusiasm, might easily transform their ordinary school hall, courtyard, or corner of quad, into a theatre; a window can be found for Juliet. People hesitate to make the attempt, thinking that they require rich costumes and expensive scenery. But the play is the thing, thanks to Shakespeare's wonderful language and the dramatic excitement of the plots he unfolds.

COACHES

The Elizabethans were great travellers, both by water and by land; and fig. 55 shows a state coach of the period. This marks a considerable development on the medieval char shown in Vol. I. Coaches were so called because they were first made at Kotze, in Hungary, during the fifteenth century. Introduced into England about 1555, at first they were very simple in structure, and the occupants had to depend for protection from the weather on curtains; but the seating is that of the later-day coach, with seats in the boot at the sides. The seventeenth century saw important developments in the craft of coachbuilding, which we shall describe upon a later page. This drawing shows the early type of coach, before the builders had hit on the idea of suspending the body by leather braces.

55 An Elizabethan Coach

CHILDREN'S BOOKS AND GAMES

CHILDREN'S BOOKS AND NURSERY GAMES

Although, with the introduction of printing, a wide field of pleasure was opened to children, they did not reap the real benefit of this great invention before the middle of the seventeenth century. Printing was still so costly and books so precious, that few books intended primarily for children are to be found before that time. Nursery stories had always been told, handed down from generation to generation by word of mouth, and lessons were taught in the same way. Quite tiny children learned to recite the Psalms in Latin, the *Gloria in Excelsis*, the Nicene Creed, and the *Paternoster*. Everything children knew had to be learned by heart. At the end of the fifteenth century, however, the earliest form of school-book, namely the horn-book, came into use. This was merely an oblong piece of wood, shaped like a battledore, on which was pasted a paper printed with the alphabet in black-letter, or in Roman characters, the numerals, or the *Ave* and the *Paternoster*. It was covered by a sheet of transparent horn, and bound at the edge with brass. It had a wooden handle, with a hole and string to hang it round the waist or neck. At the beginning of the alphabet was a little cross, and on some was written the rhyme

> Christe's cross be my speede
> In all vertue to proceede.

Because of this, children called it their criss-cross row. Some of these horn-books had backs of embossed and gilded leather. One can be seen, held by a little girl of the seventeenth century, in fig. 65.

As for nursery tales and games, nearly all our well-known fairy-tales are very old indeed. *Beauty and the Beast* had its origin, scholars believe, in a legend called the *Red Bull of Norroway*, and is either Saxon or earlier. *Jack the Giant-Killer* and *Tom Thumb* are supposed to have been taken from the legends of King Arthur. Dolls are equally old, and were bought largely at the big fairs held all over the country. At St. Bartholomew's Fair, established in 1133, there were stalls for the sale of toys, sweets and dolls; and until recent days dolls were often called "Bartholomew babies". The toys would be drums, hobby-horses, popguns and kites; and we also read of lambs made of white wool spangled with gold, the head of composition and the cheeks painted red, with black spots for eyes. These lambs had horns and legs of tin, and a piece of pink tape for the neckband. Trumpets were sold, made of cows' horns, as well as hoops, battledores and shuttlecocks, and pipes made from elder stems with the pith extracted. Boys could buy popguns firing clay pellets; and gilt gingerbread and peppermint drops at twenty a penny were known as early as the fourteenth century.

PLEASURES AND PASTIMES

Thus children had plenty of choice in their toys; and we can assume that their games, like those of their elders, were very varied. The game of bowls was popular; Sir Francis Drake was playing at bowls when the Armada came in sight. Paume, a game played by the Normans, was still in existence and was the forerunner of our modern tennis. Here is a description of this game as played in 1591:

> About 3 of the clocke ten of the Earle of Hertford's servants all Somersetshire men, in a square greene court, before her Majesty's windowe, did hang up lines, squaring out the forme of a tennis-court making a crosse line in the middle. In this square they (being stript of their dublets) played five to five, with the hand-ball, at bord and cord (as they tearme it) to the great liking of her Highness.

Many grown-up sports were very cruel; and bull-baiting, bear-baiting, and cock-fighting were favourites, as was tilting at the Quintain. Schoolboys were allowed once a year on Shrove Tuesday to bring their own cocks to their school to be matched against one another in the school cockpit.

At home, girls were taught wonderful stitches in their embroidery, and began, when very young, with a sampler on which all the various stitches were practised. In the late sixteenth century, for the first time, several interesting books of patterns were published. One descriptive title runs as follows:

> Here foloweth certaine Patternes of Cutworkes; newly invented and never published before. Also sundry sorts of spots, as flowers, birdes, and fishes, etc., and will fitly serve to be wrought, some with gould, some with silke, and some with crewell in coullers [colours]; or otherwise at your pleasure. And never but once published before. Printed by Richard Shorleyker.

56 Embroidery

A kind of patterned lace worked with a needle, very popular at this date, was called *point devisé*.

An entirely new amusement that came into being in the Elizabethan era was the invention and performance of masques. Tournaments had nearly disappeared; and, although we read of "Triumphal Justs" at the Tiltyard as a feature of Elizabeth's Court, they were not nearly so frequent nor so popular as during the fifteenth century. Their place was taken by masques. The first on record took place during the reign of Henry VIII at his feast at Greenwich in 1513. The chronicle describes it thus:

> On the daie of the Epiphanie at night, the Kynge with xi. others wer disguised after the manner of Italie called a maske, a thing not seen afore in England; they wer appareled in garments long and brode wrought all with gold, with visers and cappes of gold.

Queen Elizabeth made many progresses through the country; and, at each stopping-place, she was welcomed with a pageant and masque, generally embodying stories of the ancient gods and goddesses. At one place, where she halted beside a river, the bushes parted, and Father Neptune with attendant nymphs appeared and recited a long poem hailing her as Queen of the Seas. On another occasion, she found a great pageant was awaiting her, with Venus in the midst, who also recited verses, handing over her sceptre of beauty to the Queen! An interesting account of the Queen's visit to a private house is given in a letter written by Sir Robert Sidney, younger brother of Sir Philip Sidney, in 1600.

57 A Countrywoman

> Her Highness [he relates] hath done honour to my poor house by visiting me, and seemed much pleased at what we did to please her. My son made her a fair speech, to which she did give a most gracious reply. The women did dance before her, whilst the cornets did salute from the gallery; she did vouchsafe to eat two morsels of rich comfit cake, and drank a small cordial from a gold cup. She had a marvellous suit of velvet borne by four of her first women attendants in rich apparel; two ushers did go before, and at going upstairs she called for a staff, and was much wearied in walking about the house, and said she wished to come another day. Six drums and six trumpets waited in the court, and sounded at her approach and departure. My wife did bear herself in wondrous good liking, and was attired in a purple kyrtle, fringed with gold; and myself in rich band and collar of needlework, and did wear a goodly stuff of the bravest cut and fashion with an under-body of silver and loops. The Queen was much in commendation

58 Elizabethan Pages

of our appearances, and smiled at the ladies, who in their dances often came up to the steps on which the seat was fixed, to make their obeysance, and so fell back into their order again. The younger Markham did several gallant feats on a horse before the gate, leaping down and kissing his sword, and then mounting swiftly on the saddle, and passed a lance with much skill. The day well-nigh spent, the Queen went and tasted a small beverage that was set out in divers rooms where she might pass; and then in much order was attended to the Palace, the cornets and trumpets sounding through the streets. One knight (I dare not name) did say, the Queen had done me more honour than some that had served her better; but envious tongues have venomed shafts, and so I rest in peace with what has happened; and God speed us all, my worthy Knight.

At another pageant performed before Queen Elizabeth, there was a sham fight between two bands of men established in mock castles, built on the Temple fields at Warwick. In this fight "mortyr-pieces, and calibers, and harquebuyces, fireworks, squibs, and balls of fire" were used. So realistic was the firing that a house in the village was set on fire and completely burned down. Fireworks had just come into use; and elsewhere we are told of a sham fort overthrown by a dragon "flieing and casting out huge flames and squibs and alighting on the fort set fyere therein".

The Elizabethan era was a famous period for feasts and merry-making, when Englishmen, rich and poor, played as vigorously as they worked. Nearly all feast days had their own particular ceremony. At Hok Tide, the men of Coventry took part in a tilting match representing, in dumb show, the defeat of the Danes by the English; and on Corpus Christi Day, June 14th—again in Coventry—miracle plays and stories from the Old Testament were performed on wheeled stages which were drawn about the streets. The plays were written in rhyme. Of May Day and the morris dance more must be said later on; but here a description of an Elizabethan wedding may not come amiss.

First came the bridegroom with the young bachelors, each with bride lace upon branches of green broom tied to his left arm. . . . Then the bride, being attired in a gown of sheep's russet, and a kirtle of fine worsted, attired with abillement of gold, and her hair, as yellow as gold, hanging down behind her, which was curious

59 A Sixteenth-century Game, "Club Kayles"

> combed and plaited; she was led to church between two sweet boys, with bride laces and rosemary tied about their silken sleeves. There was fair bride-cup of silver gilt carried before her, wherein was a goodly branch of rosemary, gilded and very fair, hung about with silken ribands of all colours. Musicians came next, then a group of maidens, some bearing great bridecakes, others of garlands of wheat finely gilded; and thus they passed into the church.

Shakespeare's *Taming of the Shrew* contains a reference to the custom by which all the guests drank of the "bride-cup" in the church.

Fig. 59 shows a game popular from very early times. Today we call it "Ninepins"; but then it went by the name of "Keyles" or "Kayles"; and if, as in our picture, the pins were aimed at with a stick instead of a ball, it was called "Club Kayles". Bets were often laid on the game; and in some lines of advice to apprentices, written in the fifteenth century, they are warned to

> Exchewe allewey eville company
> Kayles, carding, and haserdy.

ELIZABETHAN ORNAMENT

Our tailpiece depicts a panel of sixteenth-century ornament, which, like the architecture of the day, was a mixture of old and new. Elizabethan designers were fond of using some central feature such as a lion's head, and taking from it straps, or bands, raised above a background with curling edges, the strap often piercing them, and finishing with pretty shaped ends. Another characteristic device involved cutting out a fretted pattern, and mounting on parts of it diamond- and oval-shaped lozenges. This sort of ornament continued into the reign of James I.

60 Sixteenth-century Ornament

Dates	Kings and Queens of England and France	Famous Men	Great Events	Principal Buildings
1602	. . . . . .	Cardinal Mazarin *b.*		Burton Agnes, Yorks., 1602–10
1603	James I, *m.* Anne of Denmark			Audley End, Essex, 1603–16
1605	. . . . . .	Sir Thomas Browne *b.*—W.	Gunpowder Plot	Bramshill, Hants, 1605–12
1606	. . . . . .	Rembrandt van Ryn *b.*—P.		Holland House
1607	. . . . . .	. . . . . .	Colonization of Virginia	
1608	. . . . . .	John Milton *b.*—Pt.		
1610	*Louis XIII of France*	Teniers the younger *b.*—P.		Wadham College, Oxford, 1610–13
1611	. . . . . .	John Webb *b.*—A.		Hatfield House
1612	. . . . . .	Samuel Butler *b.*—W.		
1613	. . . . . .	. . . . . .	. . . . . .	Bolsover Castle
1617	. . . . . .	. . . . . .	Voyage of Sir Walter Raleigh to Guiana	
1618	. . . . . .	Richard Lovelace *b.*—Pt. Sir Peter Lely *b.*—P. Murillo *b.*—P.	Voyage of the *Mayflower*	Aston Hall, Warwickshire, 1618–35
1619	. . . . . .	. . . . . .	. . . . . .	Blickling Hall, Norfolk, 1619–20
1620	. . . . . .	John Evelyn *b.*—W.		
1621	. . . . . .	Andrew Marvell *b.*—Pt.	Impeachment of Bacon	
1622	. . . . . .	Molière *b.*—W.		Banqueting Hall, Whitehall
1625	Charles I, *m.* Henrietta Maria of France		Expedition to Cadiz	
1626	. . . . . .	. . . . . .	. . . . . .	St. Peter's, Rome, dedicated, 1626
1627	. . . . . .	. . . . . .	War with France	Abbot's Hospital, Guildford
1628	. . . . . .	John Bunyan *b.*—W.	Petition of Right	
1629	. . . . . .	. . . . . .	Dissolution of Third Parliament	
1630	. . . . . .	Pieter de Hoogh *b.*—P.		Swakeleys House, Uxbridge
1631	. . . . . .	John Dryden *b.*—Pt.		S. M. della Salute, Venice
1632	. . . . . .	Samuel Pepys *b.*—W. Christopher Wren *b.*—A.		
1633	. . . . . .	Thomas Flatman (miniaturist) *b.*	Laud, Archbishop of Canterbury	
1634	. . . . . .	. . . . . .	First Levy of Ship-Money	Burford Priory Chapel
1636	. . . . . .	. . . . . .	. . . . . .	Raynham House, Norfolk
1637	. . . . . .	. . . . . .	Trial of Hampden	Oriel College, Oxford
1638	. . . . . .	Meindert Hobbema *b.*—P.	The Covenant	
1640	. . . . . .	William Wycherley *b.*—W.		Clare College Bridge
1641	. . . . . .	. . . . . .	Impeachment and execution of Strafford	
1642	. . . . . .	Sir Isaac Newton *b.*—W.	Attempted arrest of five members and Civil War	
1643	*Louis XIV of France*		Siege of Gloucester	
1644	. . . . . .	William Penn *b.*	Battle of Marston Moor	
1645	. . . . . .	. . . . . .	Battle of Naseby	
1646	. . . . . .	Sir Godfrey Kneller *b.*—P.	King joins Scots at Newark	
1647	. . . . . .	. . . . . .	King is given up to Parliament. Escapes to Carisbrooke	
1648	. . . . . .	Grinling Gibbons *b.*—S.	Second Civil War. Pride's Purge	Wilton House
1649	Oliver Cromwell		Trial and execution of the King	
1650	. . . . . .	. . . . . .	Defeat of Montrose. Battle of Dunbar	Ashburnham House
1651	. . . . . .	Thomas Otway *b.*—Pt.	Charles II invades England	
1652	. . . . . .	. . . . . .	War with Holland	
1653	. . . . . .	. . . . . .	The Protectorate	
1654	. . . . . .	. . . . . .	. . . . . .	Thorpe Hall, Northants.
1655	. . . . . .	. . . . . .	Treaty with France	
1656	. . . . . .	. . . . . .	. . . . . .	Tyttenhanger, Herts.
1658	. . . . . .	Purcell *b.*—M.	Death of Cromwell. His son Protector	
1659	. . . . . .	. . . . . .	Quarrels between Parliament and Army	
1660	Charles II, *m.* Catherine of Braganza		Monk marches on London	
1661	. . . . . .	Daniel Defoe *b.*—W.	Charles's First Parliament	
1664	. . . . . .	Matthew Prior *b.*—Pt.		Versailles
1665	. . . . . .	. . . . . .	Great Plague	Ashdown House, Berkshire
1666	. . . . . .	Sir John Vanbrugh *b.*—A.	Fire of London	Brasenose College Chapel
1667	. . . . . .	Swift *b.*—W.	Dutch on The Thames, and the Peace of Breda	Trinity College Chapel, Oxford
1668	. . . . . .	. . . . . .	The Triple Alliance	
1670	. . . . . .	Congreve *b.*—W.	Treaty of Dover	St. Catherine College, Cambridge, 1670–80
1671	. . . . . .	Colley Cibber *b.*—W.		
1672	. . . . . .	Addison *b.*—W.	Second Dutch War	St. Stephen's, Walbrook, 1672–79
1673	. . . . . .	. . . . . .	Test Act. Fall of the Cabal	Brewers' Hall
1674	. . . . . .	Isaac Watts *b.*—Hymn W.		Middle Temple, 1674–84
1675	. . . . . .	. . . . . .	. . . . . .	St. Paul's Cathedral begun
1676	. . . . . .	Richard Steele *b.*—W.		
1677	. . . . . .	. . . . . .	Marriage of William of Orange and Princess Mary	
1678	. . . . . .	Lord Bolingbroke *b.*	The Popish Plot	Trinity College Library, Cambridge
1679	. . . . . .	Thomas Parnell *b.*—Pt.	Habeas Corpus Act	
1680	. . . . . .	. . . . . .	. . . . . .	Invalides, Paris
1682	. . . . . .	. . . . . .	. . . . . .	Chelsea Hospital
1683	. . . . . .	. . . . . .	The Rye House Plot	Town Hall, Guildford
1684	. . . . . .	. . . . . .	. . . . . .	Hall, Winchester College
1685	James II, *dep.* 1688; *m.* (1) Anne Hyde; (2) Mary of Modena	John Sebastian Bach *b.*—M Handel *b.*—M.	Insurrection of Monmouth. Battle of Sedgemoor	
1687	. . . . . .	. . . . . .	Declaration of Indulgence	
1688	. . . . . .	Alexander Pope *b.*—Pt.	Invitation to William of Orange	Bluecoat School, Westminster
1689	William III, *m.* Mary of England	Richardson *b.*—W.		Hampton Court, 1689–1700
1694	. . . . . .	Earl of Chesterfield *b.*		
1695	. . . . . .	. . . . . .	. . . . . .	Greenwich Hospital
1697	. . . . . .	William Hogarth *b.*—P.		
1699	. . . . . .	Joseph Chardin *b.*—P.		

A.=Architect. P.=Painter. Pt.=Poet. S.=Sculptor. W.=Writer. M.=Musician.

61 Chart of the "Stuart" Period of Design, from 1600 to 1699

62 A Horseman of the Time of Charles II

Chapter II

SEVENTEENTH CENTURY

IT cannot be claimed that the Stuart period fulfilled the promise of the end of the sixteenth century. When Elizabeth died, conditions seemed to point to peaceful and happy days ahead. The Tudors had done their job magnificently, and when their line came to an end England stood well with the world; we had produced a race of men whose names still make the blood tingle. Yet, within a few years, the seeds of civil war had already been sown.

When James I came to the throne in 1603, he suffered from the disadvantage of not being a native Englishman. Today Scots, Irish, Welsh, and English pull together and think of Great Britain as a single realm; but not so the men of the seventeenth century, with ages of border strife behind them. They regarded James as an impoverished foreign heir succeeding to a rich inheritance. He could not carry on the intimate rule of the Tudors. Nor did the fact that his mother, Mary Queen of Scots, had met her death in England encourage him to trust his new subjects.

James's son, Charles I, was equally handicapped—both by lack of understanding and by want of tact. He failed to grasp that a people so much alive, and so much interested in affairs, as the Englishmen of the early seventeenth century, would insist on their fair share in the government of the kingdom. A collision was inevitable; and it cost the King his life. Yet, as we read through family papers, despite social unrest and civil war, we gain the impression that, except in districts immediately affected, and allowing for the poverty and difficulties caused by the struggle, life jogged on in the country districts pretty much as it had always done.

We read many accounts of gardens of flowers, fruit and vegetables; and Mr. Isham writes to Lady Verney that he will do up and send her sugar for preserving, "if she hath currants e'now for this last wick of winds hath been so big that most of them are blowed off the trees". We read also of stew ponds of fish to be cleaned out and requests to the farmer to set the decoy for wild fowl. Households did not change much; gentlewomen, if unmarried, became "helps and gentlewomen" to their relations; for the ladies of the house were still expected to superintend, and if necessary take part in, all the labours of the household. Gervase Markham's *English Housewife*, published 1631, bears the following advertisement upon its title page:

> The English housewife, containing the inward and outwards vertues which ought to be in a compleat woman. As her skill in Physick, Chirurgery, Cookery, extraction of oils, banquetting stuff, ordering of great feasts, preserving of all sorts of wines, conceited secrets, distillations of perfumes, ordering of wool, hemp or flax, making cloth and dying, the knowledge of dairies, the office of malting, of oats, their excellent uses in families, of brewing, baking and all other things belonging to a household.

Scanning this formidable list, one is bound to agree that the mistress of the household would have needed all the help that she could get from her unmarried relations. Large households were still more or less self-supporting; and cooking was on the same generous scale as in the sixteenth century.

Now that sugar was cultivated in the West Indies, it began to take the place once occupied by honey; and from the sugar-cane was distilled a drink largely used on the ships of the British Navy —"a hot hellish and terrible liquor [writes a contemporary critic] called rum". Gin was also distilled, so called because it was flavoured with juniper. One innovation that benefited country housewives was the local carrier's cart, which ran through many districts twice a week; and from some large places—Tonbridge for one—the post (by coach) went to London every day. Roads were still bad; lawlessness was rife. An effort was made to cope with the hordes of beggars by issuing, in each parish, to sundry poor persons unable to earn their living, badges giving them licence to beg, those begging without these badges to be imprisoned and otherwise punished. Men who tramped the country to sell their goods were given hawkers' licences as an assurance of their genuineness. Yet, in the time of Charles I, a kind of market grew up at the entrance to the palace precincts which became the scene of such confusion, noise and squalor, that a rule limiting it was made; officers were ordered to ride through the mob of hucksters and retainers and arrest all disorderly persons.

Meanwhile legitimate trade was fast increasing. The East India Company was founded in 1600; and younger sons of prosperous families were often sent abroad to study some particular branch of commerce. Thus one of the young Verneys went to France, and another to Spain for the purpose of learning the leather trade. The Vauxhall glassworks were opened in 1670, where workmen brought from Venice blew glass and made mirrors.

COSTUME

Our study of the everyday things of the period once again begins with costume. During the reign of James I, bombasted breeches and the monstrous farthingale were still worn; but with Charles I came a sudden reaction. The first man in fig. 117 is a seventeenth-century Cavalier. His dress is rich, but simpler than that of the Elizabethan Age. His hair is long, and the ruff has given place to a large lace-edged collar and cuffs. His coat fits loosely to the figure, and is braided and tagged round the waist. These tags were silken laces fastened to the breeches beneath, and drawn through eyelet holes in the tunic and knotted above. They answered the purpose of braces; stockings were fastened to breeches in the same way. Sleeves were cut to show the shirt beneath, and a wide cloak was worn. Breeches were still full, but no longer padded, and two pairs of stockings

63 A Schoolmaster, 1631

were often worn—the outer pair shorter than the inner, and edged with lace, which showed above the top of the wide boot.

Ear-rings were fancied by the young beaux, who even painted their faces. The following is an account of a little boy's clothes. His age was eight. He wore for winter a baize gown faced with fur; for high days, his suit was of ash-coloured satin, doublet hose, stockings with silk garters and roses all to match, with an embroidered girdle and a cloak of the same colour, trimmed with squirrel fur. He had also a taffeta pickadel and ruff, and his sword was fastened with a green scarf. He wore out five pairs of shoes in a year.

Ladies' skirts, although full, were no longer extended on a frame, but were caught back to show an embroidered petticoat underneath. Satin and stiff silk, or velvet, were largely used for the dresses, which were cut low on the shoulder, and finished with a delicate muslin and lace collar, with cuffs to match. Long gauntlet gloves were largely worn; and fashionable ladies sometimes wore as many as three pairs, one on top of the other, each pair beautifully embroidered. The hair was drawn off the face into a knot behind, and the side pieces fell in ringlets on to the shoulders. Masks were always worn by the Court ladies in public; it was considered immodest to appear without one. Hence the term "barefaced".

Our second man is a Puritan—one of those devout persons whose protest against fashionable follies took the form of wearing deliberately unfashionable clothes. See his plain hat without a feather, his closely cropped hair, and his suit of sombre hue. Notice, too, his collar and cuffs without lace, and the lack of any trimming on his coat and breeches. From this

64 A Lady's Winter Dress, 1664

cropped head sprang the name "Roundhead", which distinguished the Puritans from the Cavaliers in the Civil War. His wife's dress is very simple too; dull in colour, lacking all trimmings, with plain collar and cuffs, and a large white apron. Fashionable women, too, occasionally wore small aprons of delicate silk and lace, though, of course, neither so large nor plain as that of a Puritan. During the Commonwealth, the more sober method of dress was general; but with Charles II came a return of fine clothes and bright colours; and, in the reaction from the dull garments of the time gone by, folks were very gay indeed. The last couple belong to this time. The lady's hair is arranged in masses of ringlets; but sometimes elderly women wore wigs, much curled, and standing up high above the forehead.

65 A little Schoolgirl holding her Horn-book, 1667

Bodices were peaked; and the full sleeves were open in front and caught together with jewelled clasps. Skirts were wide and dresses were made of beautiful materials, either satins or rich silks.

The lady wears a wide cloak, held with a jewel on one shoulder; and out of doors she would have had a large hooded cloak, or sometimes a hood alone. Pepys says in 1665: "To church, it being Whit-Sunday;

my wife, very fine in a new yellow bird's-eye hood as the fashion is now." Masks have gone out of fashion.

"I now observed," writes John Evelyn in 1654, "that Women began to paint themselves, formerly a most ignominious thing."

Again, in his diary of 1666, he gives us some idea of the costume that ladies assumed when they went out riding: "The Queen was now in her Cavalier riding habit, hat and feathers and horseman's coat, going to take the air." Pepys gives us a more detailed account:

66 A Sweep, 1688

> Walking in the galleries at Whitehall I find the Ladies of Honour dressed in their riding garbs, with coats and doublets with deep skirts, just for all the world like mine; and buttoned in their doublets up to the breast, with periwiggs and with hats; so that, only for a long petticoat dragging under their men's coats, nobody could take them for women in any point whatever; which was an odd sight.

On the third man, we see that the tunic of Charles I's reign has given place to garments that are the origin of the modern coat and waistcoat, and that his sleeves are no longer slit, but are turned back at three-quarter length with wide cuffs, showing his full shirt sleeves, edged at the wrist with a frill. Wide collars had gone out of fashion and were replaced by a small lace cravat. Men carried muffs in the street; and we read in *Pepys's Diary* that he took his wife's muff for his own use and bought her a new one—just the sort of thing the old villain would do. Breeches, edged with a deep lace frill and rosetted at the knee, were of the same colour as the coat. Stockings and shoes replaced high boots, and shoes were long, narrow, buckled, and square in the toe. Wigs, long and much curled, were seen on every man. It is said that they came into fashion with the Restoration; for many men with the cropped head of the Commonwealth wished to conceal their former principles and were desirous of imitating as nearly as possible the Cavalier love-locks.

67 A small boy of 1633

Little boys usually wore long coats, nearly reaching to their ankles; but, when they were put into coat and waistcoat, they were often obliged to wear corsets to make their long straight waistcoats set well.

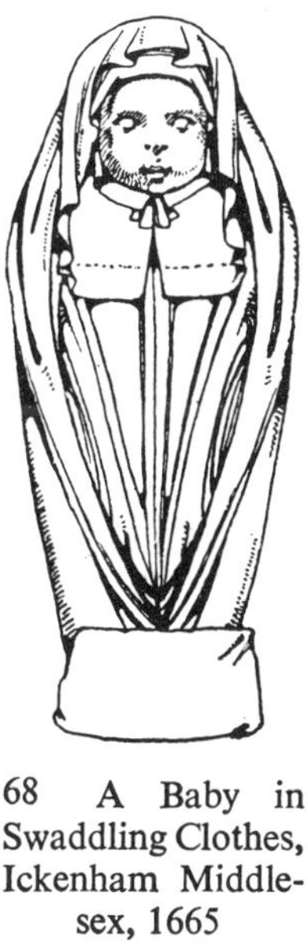

68 A Baby in Swaddling Clothes, Ickenham Middlesex, 1665

A charming letter, written in the late seventeenth century, and preserved in the *Lives of the Norths*, describes the breeching of a little six-year-old boy named Frank:

> You cannot beleeve the great concerne that was in the whole family here, last Wednesday, it being the day that the taylor was to helpe to dress little Frank in his breeches, in order to the making an everyday suit by it. Never had any bride that was to be drest upon her wedding night more hands about her, some the legs and some the arms, the taylor butt'ning, and others putting on the sword, and so many lookers on, that, had I not a ffinger amongst them I could not have seen him. . . . They are very fitt, everything, and he looks taller and prettyer than in his coats [petticoats].

69 A Widow of 1632

Little Charles reyoiced as much as he did, for he jumpt all the while about him, and took notice of everything. I went to Bury and bo't everything for another suitt which will be finisht upon Saturday. So the coats are to be quite left of on Sunday. . . . When he was drest he asked Buckle whether muffs were out of fashion because they had not sent him one.

Fig. 67 shows the dress of a small boy of 1633, before he was breeched. His tunic and skirt are of scarlet trimmed with gold; and he has a white lawn collar and cuffs, and undersleeves of the same material which shows inside the open outer sleeve. Fig. 68 shows a baby in swaddling clothes taken from a tomb, dated 1665, in Ickenham Church. Fig. 69 is the portrait of a widow, dated 1632.

Mourning was made the occasion of great ceremony and the rules regarding mourning were rigid. Black bed-hangings were considered necessary; and the Verney family in 1650 owned a great black bed that went the rounds of the family as deaths occurred. Mourning was sent to intimate friends as well as to relations. A black coach—that is, a coach covered with a black cloth—was used, the servants' saddles also being covered in black.

SHIPS AND SHIPBUILDING

The seventeenth century witnessed some notable developments in shipbuilding. But, if the ships were better, the sailors, with a few exceptions, do not compare favourably with those of the sixteenth century. We know a great deal of their doings thanks to the diary kept by Samuel Pepys, between 1660 and 1669, when he was a clerk in the Navy Office. Later on, in 1673, he was made Secretary of the Navy, when James II, then Duke of York, was Lord High Admiral. James, very ably helped by Pepys, was a good friend to the sailors. But *Pepys's Diary*, of course, does not deal with naval affairs alone. Written in a shorthand he had invented himself—for nobody else was meant to read it—it gives us a wonderfully vivid picture of his thoughts and feelings and the adventures of his everyday life. Curious that such a private record should have become one of the most famous books in the English language!

To go back to the beginning of the century—although James I was too mean to spend money on the Navy, and was content with the laurels gained in Elizabethan times, Charles I proved more conscientious and encouraged shipbuilding. It was during his reign (1637) that the *Sovereign of the Seas* was designed by Phineas, and built by Peter Pett; and we have selected this boat for our illustration (70). Her length was 169 feet 9 inches, beam 48 feet 4 inches, and depth of hold 19 feet 4 inches, tonnage 1,683. Remember that before 1628 tonnage was reckoned by the space sufficient to stow a tun of wine—42 cubic feet. After that date, it was length of keel × greatest breadth of

70 The *Sovereign of the Seas*

beam × depth ÷ 100. The Pett family were naval architects and boat-builders from the reign of Henry VIII to that of William and Mary; and we hear about them from Pepys. The *Sovereign*, which was considered a wonderful boat, saw service under Blake. She was the first boat to carry royals and top-gallants on all masts. The cut of the sails should be noticed, and how they belly out much more largely than they did on later vessels. One lateen remains on the mizzen; but over this there are now square sails. There is a spritsail under the bowsprit, and an amusing square sail on the sprit topmast over it. The lines of the hull still show a likeness to the galley: there is the same snaky build, with beak head and high poop. John Evelyn, the other great seventeenth-century diarist, writing of the *Sovereign*, remarks that she was called the *Golden Devil* by the Dutch, owing to the amount of carving and gilding on her stern. She was remodelled in 1684 and renamed the *Royal Sovereign*, and finally was burnt at Chatham in 1696.

Though Charles at his death left the Navy weak, as an instrument in Cromwell's hands it was used to enforce respect for us abroad. The Dutch War of 1652–4 produced our great admiral, Robert Blake, who fought against Tromp and De Ruyter. But the next Dutch War of 1665–7 found us sadly unprepared: "We do nothing in this office [Pepys admitted] like people able to carry on a war." The Great Plague of 1665, of course, handicapped our efforts; but bribery and corruption was the order of the day and did far more harm. Even Pepys, who was an honest man for the time, had his price, but excuses himself, when taking a present, by not looking at it, "that I might say that I did not know what there was in the bag". The Dutch sailed up to Chatham in 1667, and burned our ships there.

This was a tragic development; for only a few years earlier British shipyards had produced the first vessel to which the name of "yacht" was given in England (71). Evelyn wrote in his diary, for October 1st, 1661: "I sailed this morning with his Majesty in one of his yachts (or pleasure boats), vessels not known among us till the Dutch East India Company presented that curious piece to the King." When Charles II was recalled to England, he had sailed to meet the English fleet in a Dutch yacht, escorted by twelve others. Charles remarked on the handiness

71 Charles II "Yaugh"

72 The Stern of the *Royal Charles*, a First Rate, built in 1673

73 The Stern of an English Second Rate of the smaller class, 1670

From Drawings by Van de Velde

of the little vessels that had been evolved on the narrow waterways of Holland. The Dutchmen, understanding that Charles, as King of England, would be a much more influential person than the impoverished exile they had known since 1649, asked him to accept a yacht then building, which was duly sent to England. Charles acknowledged the receipt of his "curious piece" in the following terms: "Maintenant vous avez encore rafraichie Nostre memoire par un nouveau present d'un Yaugh, des plus jolys et des plus agreables a nostre humeur qu'on auroit pu inventer." His letter was dated August 16th, 1660. Pepys went to see the Dutch boat with Pett, the shipbuilder, on November 8th, 1660, and noted that he was to build an English one to outdo it.

By January 13th, 1661, Pett's yacht was so far advanced that Pepys could see it, and report that it was "a pretty thing, and much beyond the Dutchman's". Later, we read of the yachts racing from Greenwich to Gravesend and back, attended by barges and kitchen boats. The Dutch boat was called *Mary*. Modern racing yachts are lineal descendants of the *Mary*.

The last Dutch war of the seventeenth century was fought between 1671 and 1674; and the honours seem to have been pretty evenly divided with our sturdy foes. The most memorable result was that we gained New Amsterdam, and renamed it New York, after James, Duke of York, who later on was to be James II. The rivalry ceased with the accession of William and Mary. Evelyn has a note in his diary in 1683, that shows how bad was our naval position at the end of Charles II's reign:

> This summer did we suffer twenty French men-of-war to pass our Channel towards the Sound, to help the Danes against the Swedes, who had abandoned the French interest; we not having ready sufficient to guard our coasts or take cognizance of what they did; though the nation never had more, or a better navy, yet the sea had never so slender a fleet.

The diary of Henry Teonge throws some interesting sidelights on life in the Navy. A Navy chaplain between 1675 and 1679, he must have been a sporting parson. Although he was fifty-four when he first went to sea, "no life at the shoare", he declared, was "comparable to this at sea, where we have good meate and good drinke provided for us, and good company, and good divertisments; without the least care, sorrow or trouble"; which sounds as if his previous existence had been hard. His first trip was in the *Assistance*. They started from the Thames, and at Dover the captain's wife, and other ladies, were put ashore "with 3 cheares, 7 guns, and our trumpets sounding". This practice led to a regulation:

> Forasmuch as the Harbouring of Women and Children on board his Ma[tie] Shipps in Ordinary may expose them to accidents . . . as well as Inconveniences of other kinds, We doe hereby strictly forbid the Lodgeing or keeping of any Women or Children on board the sd. Shipps on any pretence whatsoever.

Teonge's description of the food is quite appetising. Off Lisbon,

> our noble Capt. feasted the officers of his small squadron with 4 dishes of meate, viz., 4 excellent henns and a peice of pork boyled, in a dish; a giggett of excellent mutton and turnips; a peice of beife of 8 ribbs, well seasoned and roasted; and a couple of very fatt greene geese; last of all a greate chesshyre cheese.

As they drank "Canary, Sherry, Renish, Clarett, white wine, syder, ale, beare and punch", one understands why the Captain is described as "noble". The ordinary seamen's food was bread or biscuit, beer, beef, pork, peas, oatmeal, flour, suet, butter, and cheese.

At Gibraltar, "every on that hath not yet beene in the Straites pays his dollar, or must be duckt at yard arme". Strict discipline was maintained; on Monday mornings, boys who had misbehaved during the week past were "whipt with a catt with 9 tayles for their misdemeanours, by the boarson's mate". Again, two men and a boy had "an iron pinn clapt closse into their mouths, and tyd behind their heads; and there they stood a whole houre . . . an excellent cure for swearers"—if a rather rough one.

The *Assistance* helped at the blockade of Tripoli, and the boatswain died.

> He had a neate coffin, which was covered over with on of the King's jacks, and his boarson's sylver whisle and chaine layd on the top betweene 2 pistolls crost with a hangar drawne. At his going off the ship he had 9 gunns, which were fyred at a minut's distance. And 8 trompetts sownding dolefully, whereof the 4 in the first ranke began and the next 4 answered, so that ther was a continued dolefull tone from the ship to the shoare, and from

> thence to the grave. Halfe the ship's company, with their musketts in the right posture, going after the corps, with all the officers of all the ships that were there. . . . When he was buryed he had 4 peales of muskett shott. And as soone as we were out of the church yard the trumpetts sounded merry levitts all the way.

On Christmas Day aboard ship, the trumpeters tuned up outside the cabin doors, "playing a levitc at each cabine doore, and bidding good morrow, wishing a merry Christmas"; for dinner they "had excellent good fayre; a ribb of beife, plumb puddings, minct pyes". On Twelfth Night

> wee had a greate kake made, in which was put a beane for the King, a pease for the Queen, a cloave for the knave, a ragg for the slutt. The kake was cutt into severall peices in the great cabin, and all putt into a napkin, out of which every on took his peice as out of a lottery: then each peice is broaken to see what was in it, which caused much laughter.

What pleasant people these old sailors were!

The same festivities on land have been described by Robert Herrick, who lived from 1591 to 1674, in a poem entitled "Twelfe night, or King and Queene". Here are two verses:

> Now, now the mirth comes
> With the cake full of plums,
> Where Beane's the King of the sport here:
> Beside we must know,
> The Pea also
> Must revell, as Queene, in the Court here.
>
> Begin then to chuse,
> (This night as ye use)
> Who shall for the present delight here,
> Be a King by the lot,
> And who shall not
> Be Twelfe-day Queene for the night here.

To return to seafaring life, however, it was in the reign of William and Mary that Greenwich Hospital was founded as a home for aged seamen, and built from the design of Sir Christopher Wren. John Evelyn was the first Treasurer. Meanwhile, attention began to be paid to lighting the coasts. The first Eddystone Lighthouse was built 1694–8, but was destroyed by a great storm in 1703. Fig. 74 shows that it was a somewhat

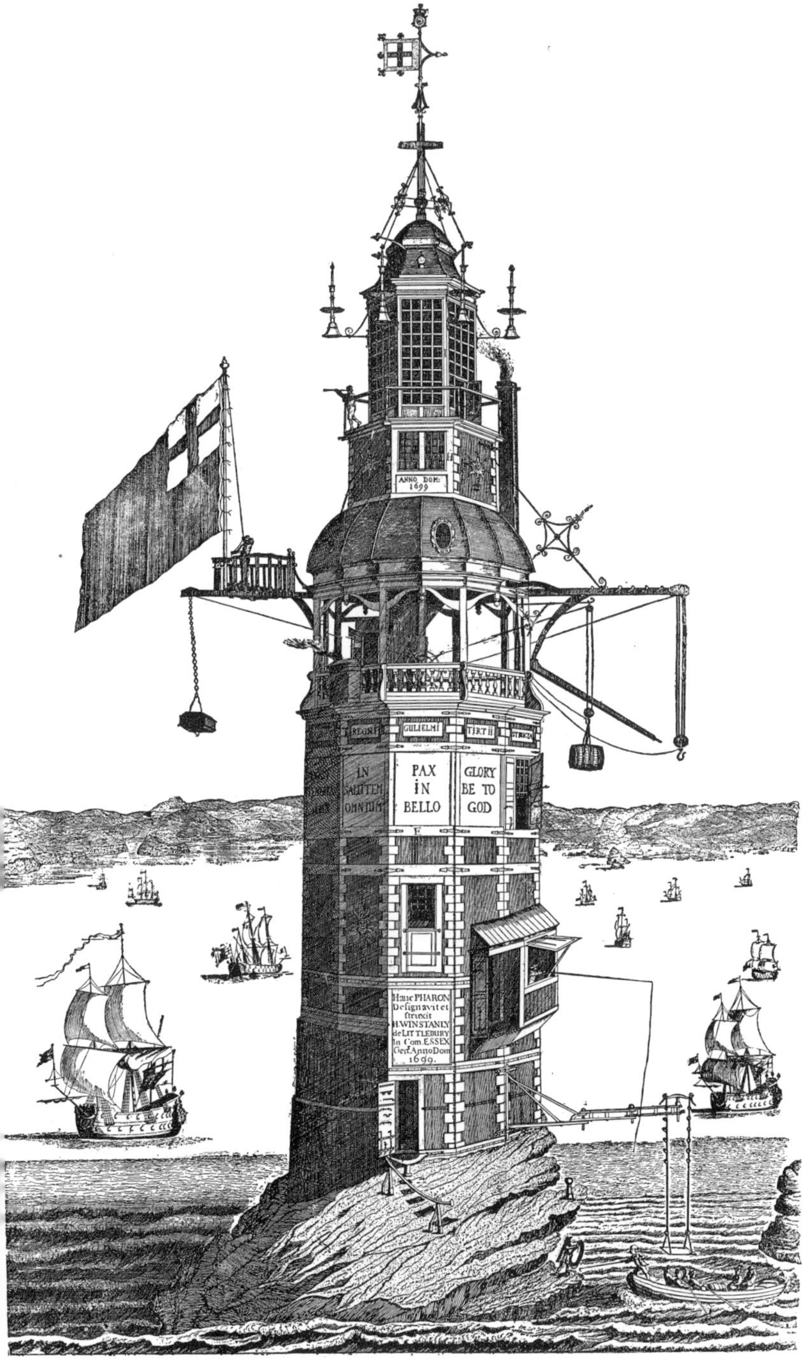

74 The first Eddystone Lighthouse, designed by Henry Winstanley.
Destroyed by Storm, 1703

From an Engraving by the Designer

fantastic pile, recalling a Chinese pagoda. Its design and erection were due to a curious character, Henry Winstanley, engraver and engineer, of Essex, whose charming little house at Littlebury, near Saffron Walden, is shown in fig. 76. He engraved a whole set of plates of Audley End, in Essex, which are particularly valuable as they show a great court that has since utterly vanished. He also engraved a fine Tudor house at Rycote, Oxfordshire, which has almost entirely disappeared. When working on the lighthouse, he was carried off by a French privateer and his work destroyed; but he was exchanged for a French prisoner and returned to finish it. He always said he wished above all else to be in it during a great storm; and his wish was fulfilled, in the great tempest of November 27th, 1703. When the tempest had passed, nothing was left of this Heath Robinson erection or of its designer and his five companions. The versatile Winstanley also specialised in hydraulic devices, ingenious but quite useless, of which he gave displays at the "Water Theatre" in Piccadilly. His widow continued to show them, both there and at his house, as late as 1714. They included water-playing mermaids, gods and goddesses, a fiery dragon belching forth fireballs, and a "Curious Barrel" which spouted all sorts of pleasant drinks.

THE SEVENTEENTH-CENTURY HOUSE

Once again we return to domestic architecture. Fig. 75 shows a house of the middle of Charles I's reign. That monarch was a great patron of the arts, and one of the first to start a collection of pictures. With his French wife, he probably led the way, and helped to make fashionable the new Renaissance style of architecture, of which we saw the beginnings in the last century. This particular house is interesting because, where its exterior is concerned, it is not very far ahead of such houses as Blickling and Hatfield, built in James I's reign. It is still gabled, though the gables have, as terminations, the classical feature called a pediment; the general outline then follows traditional lines, though the detail is more scholarly than before. The windows were originally glazed with leaded lights in the form of casements, hinged at the side like doors, not as sashes sliding up and down; but they were grouped in a different way from those of the sixteenth century. This example was converted to the

75 A House of the Time of Charles I

Drawing founded on Raynham Hall, Norfolk

76 Winstanley's House at Littlebury, Essex

sash type of window when it was altered by William Kent about 1730.

The first Eaton Hall, Chester(79), erected about the end of the century, shows a further development towards the classic style. It is a pleasing, restrained design, with two large kitchen and stable blocks set at right angles.

When we reach the inside of the house we find that, though the exterior has points of resemblance with Blickling and Hatfield, the interior reveals great changes—so much so that, perhaps for the first and only time in one of our illustrations, the architecture and dress of the period do not go together: the latter has a distinctly old-fashioned look. It may be that the owner, Sir Roger Townshend, who was largely his own architect, wished the outside of his house to be homely, but did not object to the interior being fashionable. Actually, most of the inside had to be finished later on(77).

Inigo Jones, who did work of this character, was born in 1573 and died 1652, and must be reckoned as the first important English architect. Thorpe, who lived in the reigns of Elizabeth and James, was working as early as 1570, and Smithson, who died in 1634, have left collections of drawings of houses. But they must be regarded as representative of the old school of architecture, in which a group of men joined forces to produce a single building, each designing his own part of a traditional

77 The Hall of a Seventeenth-century House

Founded on the Hall at Raynham Hall, Norfolk. The Ceiling is later in date

treatment, while the chief architect—Thorpe or Smithson—supplied the general layout. Jones, and his kinsman and pupil Webb, and the later architects, designed the whole; and their work was good and scholarly, if somewhat lacking in the interest of the earlier period.

> Being naturally inclined in my younger years [wrote Inigo Jones], to study the arts of design, I passed into foreign parts to converse with the great masters thereof in Italy, where I applied myself to search out the Ruins of those ancient Buildings, which, in despite of Time itself and violence of Barbarians, are yet remaining. Having satisfied myself in these, and returning to my native country, I applied my mind more particularly to the study of Architecture.

A second visit was paid in 1613–14. So Inigo Jones was well equipped when he designed the Banqueting Hall in Whitehall, which was finished in 1622. Fully classical in style and modelled on the "Ruins of those ancient Buildings" which Jones had seen in Italy, it was the first structure of its kind in England. As such, it is an astonishing production, and the fruit of great mental effort—but then, Inigo Jones was undoubtedly a man of genius.

The Banqueting Hall, however, is only a small fragment of the vast scheme for the Palace of Whitehall, a design of stupendous magnificence, prepared largely by Inigo Jones's nephew, John Webb.

The Saloon of Raynham Hall(77) is a restrained classic design, remarkable for its deeply recessed ceiling modelled in high relief, with painted panels. This probably remains more or less as it was originally built, though the cornice, chimneypiece, and ceiling paintings are due to William Kent, who is responsible for practically all the other interiors

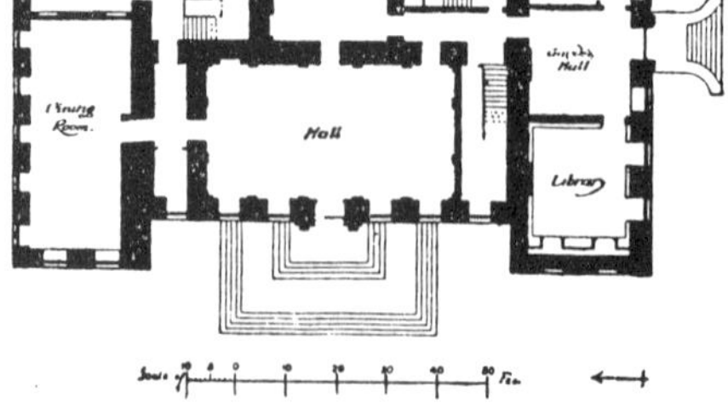

78 A Plan of Raynham Hall

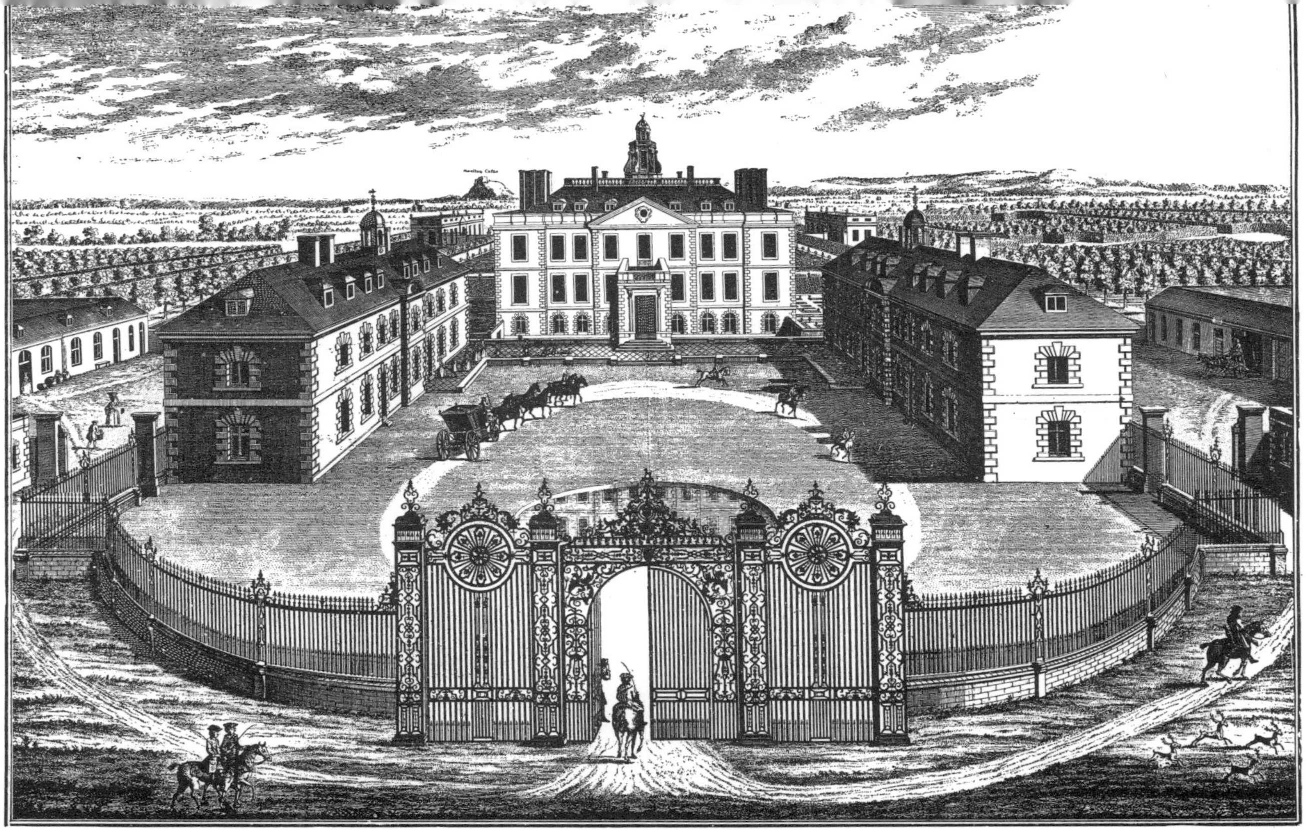

79 The first Eaton Hall, Cheshire, close of the Seventeenth Century, with Ironwork by the Brothers Roberts

From an Engraving by T. Badeslade

in the house. They are good designs in the Palladian style, dating just about a hundred years after the house was actually erected. Jones created a very beautiful double cube room at Wilton about 1649.

The plan of the house(78) again marks a definite change. The hall now becomes a place of entrance only, and the whole arrangement is more modern in treatment. The kitchen and servants have been banished to the basement; and master and man no longer meet on common ground.

WREN AND RENAISSANCE CHURCH-BUILDING

Sir Christopher Wren was a worthy successor to Jones and Webb. Born in 1632, he first attracted attention as an astronomer and mathematician, and turned to architecture later. Wren carried out the construction of the Sheldonian Theatre at Oxford between 1663 and 1668. In the latter year he was appointed Surveyor to His Majesty's Works. Webb had hoped to obtain the appointment, but was not in favour because he had been active during the Commonwealth. Wren's masterpiece, of course, is St. Paul's Cathedral; and, after the Great Fire, he built many smaller City churches, some of which were destroyed by German bombs, while others, alas, have been pulled down by his countrymen.

Groups of Renaissance churches are also to be found at Bristol and Worcester. Though not very common, there are quite a number of Renaissance country churches scattered about, especially in the Midlands; and, for the first time, Mr. Marcus Whiffen has told us about them in *Stuart and Georgian Churches: 1603–1837*, published in 1948. Many of them are charming buildings, such as Ingestre in Staffordshire (possibly by Wren himself), Gayhurst, in Buckinghamshire, and Great Witley in Worcestershire. In the new countries, like America, the churches naturally conformed to a Renaissance design. In New England, for example, there are many beautiful wooden structures following the pattern of Wren's London churches; and very pretty they look, set on pleasant green lawns, and surrounded by timber-framed houses.

Figs. 80 and 81 show such a church at Willen in North Buckinghamshire, not far from Newport Pagnell. The nave and tower were built by Dr. Richard Busby, Headmaster of

80 The Interior

81 The Tower

WILLEN CHURCH, BUCKINGHAMSHIRE

Westminster School, about 1680; and it is now thought that Hooke, a collaborator of Wren, was the architect. The chambers at the side of the tower were added a few years later; and in one was housed the library presented by Dr. Busby. Both the outside of red brick and stone, and the inside, with the beautifully designed font and fine plasterwork, are thoroughly in the Wren manner, excepting only the apse, which was added in the nineteenth century. From the tower an avenue leads down to the road, across which is the parsonage. One imagines the fine figure of Dr. Busby pacing up the avenue, in his fine town clothes, to his fine town church, followed by the abashed yokels. Willen church fits its period, as all good architecture does; but perhaps the period was not a very spiritual one. Pepys was a great churchgoer, and a keen admirer of a good sermon, though somewhat apt to have his attention distracted by the presence of a pretty woman in an adjoining pew. He would have been perfectly at home in Willen, but not quite so happy in Wing or Stewkley Churches a few miles away. We give a full account of a country Greek classic church, built about a century later at Ayot St. Lawrence, Hertfordshire, in Vol. III.

While we are writing about Wren and his work, we must take the opportunity of quoting one of the love letters he wrote to Faith Coghill, who later was to become his wife. Surely it is a model of what such letters should be. Faith had dropped her watch in the water, and asked her lover to have it put right:

> MADAM,—The artificer having never before mett with a drowned Watch, like an ignorant physician has been soe long about the cure that he hath made me very unquiet that your comands should be soe long deferred; however, I have sent the watch at last and envie the felicity of it, that it should be soe neer your side, and soe often enjoy your Eye, and be consulted by you how your Time shall passe while you employ your hand in your excellent workes. But have a care of it, for I put such a Spell into it that every Beating of the Ballance will tell you 'tis the pulse of my Heart which labours so much to serve you and more Trewly than the watch; for the watch I believe will sometimes lie, and sometimes perhaps be idle and unwilling to goe, having received so much injury by being drenched in that briny bath, that I dispair it should ever be a Trew Servant to you more. But as for me (unless you drown me too in my Teares) you may be confident I shall never cease to be, Your most affectionate, humble servant, "CHR. WREN."

82 A late Seventeenth-century Dining-room
Founded on Belton House, Lincolnshire

ROOMS AND FURNITURE

Fig. 82 shows a dining-room in a typical house, built at the beginning of William and Mary's reign. This room is a fine example of the work of the period. The walls are panelled in oak right up to the ceiling, and the latter is beautifully modelled in plaster. The carving is in the style of Grinling Gibbons, who did much work for Wren.

Walls were not always panelled in wood. "Supped at my Lady Mordaunt's at Ashtead," notes Evelyn in 1665, "where was a room hung with pintado, full of figures, great and small, prettily representing sundry trades and occupations of the Indians with their habits" (pintado was printed cotton imported from the East Indies).

Now for the staircase. Once the designers had accustomed themselves to the wooden staircase, they rapidly altered and improved on it. The sixteenth-century type has two flights, side by side; and this form of construction is called "dog-legged" because the two flights together were supposed to follow the shape of a dog's leg. In the later seventeenth-century design we illustrate (83) the flights are arranged, with a better result, round a central well-hole; but the constructional details are much the same. The balustrade, formed of a pierced and vigorously carved acanthus scroll, is very decorative. This pattern was never very general; but examples are to be found at Thorpe Hall, Peterborough, built by Webb about 1650–6, Durham Castle, a house at Eltham, Kent, about 1660, and particularly fine ones at Dunster Castle and Tythrop House, Oxfordshire, which are rather later in date.

The costume of the man on the staircase is worth noting. It came suddenly into fashion in the reign of Charles II, and as suddenly disappeared a very short time after. Evelyn refers to it in his diary as "the Eastern or Persian fashion of dress"; and Pepys, in 1666, mentions it thus:

> This day the King begins to put on his vest . . . being a long cassocke close to the body, of black cloth, and pinked with white silk under it and a coat over it, and the legs ruffled with black riband like a pigeon's leg . . . but it is a very fine and handsome garment.

83 A Scroll Staircase in Charles II's Reign
In a house in Guildford High Street

Again: "the Court is all full of vests". Pepys adds an amusing scrap of gossip:

> Mr. Batelier tells me the news how the King of France hath, in defiance to the King of England, caused all his footmen to be put into vests, and that the noblemen of France will do the like.

This was probably the cause of the costume being suddenly given up in England.

The seventeenth century was a splendid period for beautiful furniture, totally different in the latter half from the Jacobean work of the earlier period. Leather carpets came into use and many chairs were upholstered.

Our next illustration (84) is of a bed, drawn to show the great height, which was characteristic of the seventeenth century. The first upholstered beds started with square tops (following the lines of the oak cornices (37)), with valances, and plumes of ostrich feathers at the angles. After the reign of Charles II cornices were attached, and grew very elaborate; but in Queen Anne's time designs again became simpler. The one illustrated is of the time of William and Mary; the cornice of the tester, or top, and the pillow board are shaped in wood, with a covering

84 A Bed of the Time of William and Mary

damask or velvet glued on. The hangings were of figured velvets, or damasks of splendid pattern. The valances were edged at first with fringes, and then later with galon or braid. Head valances are those hanging from the tester; basses, those on the bed itself; bonegraces, the curtains over the head at the back of the bed; cantonnières closed the joint at the angles of the head valances. The colour schemes were very beautiful: blue and silver, green and silver, rose and crimson damasks, olive green and rose on a cream ground.

From *Evelyn's Diary* for 1662, we learn that

> the Queen's bed was an embroidery of silver and crimson velvet, cost £8,000, being a present made by the States of Holland. . . . The great looking-glass and toilet of beaten and massive gold was given by the Queen Mother.

Pepys, in 1665, describes a bed, "where though I lay the softest I ever did in my life, with a down bed, after the Danish manner upon me, yet I slept very ill". Another entry, in 1666, is interesting: "I home late to Sir W. Pen's [his neighbour], who did give me a bed, but without curtains or hangings, all being down. So here I went the first time into a naked bed." People really needed curtains, because the rooms were being made loftier and the fireplaces were smaller than in earlier times, with the result that bedchambers were often chilly.

The Dutch influence on dress, architecture and household furnishings was very marked at this time; and a good deal of furniture was directly imported from Holland.

A TOURIST ON HORSEBACK

We will now turn to a diary which is not nearly so well known as Pepys's, but particularly interesting because it gives the woman's point of view.[1] Celia Fiennes was a lady who lived in the time of William and Mary, and journeyed up and down England on horseback. She, too, was consumed with curiosity, and, fortunately for us, wrote of all the everyday things she saw. But Celia was not at all interested in old houses; Haddon Hall and Penshurst are dismissed with a few words. What she liked

[1] *Through England on a Side Saddle* (*The Diary of Celia Fiennes*) by the Honble. Mrs. Griffiths. Field & Tuer, 1888.

was a nice new house, and she describes these as being of the "London mode".

Of Lord Chesterfield's house at Bradby, Leicestershire, she remarks: "Ye front have something surpriseing in it; its all of free stone wch is dipt in oyle that adds a varnish to its Lustre."

Beautiful furniture also attracted her attention. Here are some notes of Lord Orfford's house near Newmarket:

> The whole house is finely furnish'd with differing Coulld Damaske and velvets, some ffigured and others plaine, at Least 6 or 7 in all Richly made up after a new mode. In ye best drawing-roome was a very Rich hanging gold and silver and a Little scarlet, mostly tissue and brocade of gold and silver and border of green damaske round it; ye window Curtain ye same green damaske, and doore Curtains. There was no Looking glass but on ye Chimney piece and just opposite in ye place a looking glass used to be was 4 pannells of glass in Length and 3 in breadth set together in ye wanscoate.

Other rooms were

> well wanscoated and hung and there was ye finest Carv'd wood in fruitages, herbages, gumms, beasts, fowles, &c, very thinn and fine all in white wood with out paint or varnish. . . . There was a great flower pott Gilt Each side the chimney in the dineing Room for to sett trees in.

Another house had a billiard table.

Celia must have been a practically minded woman; for she comments on baths and details of water-supply. At Sir John St. Barbe's house, between Southampton and Romsey, she finds

> a backyard where is a Bathing house and other necessarys. . . . There is a water house that by a Wheele Casts up the Water out of ye River just by, and fills ye pipes to Serve all ye house and to fill ye bason designed in the middle of the Garden with a spout in the middle.

At Chatsworth

> there is a fine Grottoe all stone pavement Roofe and sides, this is design'd to supply all ye house with water besides severall ffanceyes to make diversion. Within this is a batheing roome, ye walls all with blew and white marble—the pavement mix'd, one stone white,

> another black, another of ye Red vaned marble. The bath is one Entire marble all white finely veined with blew and is made smooth, but had it been as finely pollish'd as some it would have been the finest marble that Could be seen. It was as deep as ones middle on the outside, and you went down steps into ye bath big enough for two people. At ye upper End are two Cocks to let in one hott, ye other Cold water to attempter it as persons please—the Windows are all private Glass.

How they heated the water we cannot say—probably in a large copper. Another amusing little note on the toilet (though not by Celia Fiennes) occurs in a letter to Sir Ralph Verney in Paris, asking him to inquire for

> the little brushes for making clean of the teeth, most covered with sylver and some few with gold and sylver twiste, together with some petits bronettes [boxes] to put them in.

Mary Verney also speaks of wooden combs being held in great esteem in London.

Great attention was paid to the design of gardens, and these generally included some hydraulic jokes. At Wilton, near Salisbury, there was a grotto in the garden

> garnished with many fine ffigures of ye Goddesses, and about 2 yards off the doore is severall pipes in a line that with a sluce spoutts water up to wett the strangers—in the middle roome is a round table and a large Pipe in the midst, on which they put a Crown or Gun or a branch, and so yt spouts the water through ye Carvings and poynts all round ye roōme at ye Artists pleasure to wet ye Company—there are figures at Each corner of ye roome that Can weep water on the beholders;

other devices brought rain from the roof. In smaller rooms water was contrived to bubble through pipes and imitate "ye melody of Nightingerlls and all sorts of birds"; but when the curiosity of strangers was engaged and they moved into the room, they were drenched with water from another line of pipes. We like to think of the seventeenth-century folk standing round waiting for the joke to come off.

Celia first saw orange trees at Sir John St. Barbe's house, and again at the Earl of Chesterfield's:

> Beyond this Garden is a Row of orange and Lemon trees set in ye ground, of a man's height and pretty big, full of flowers and some

Large fruit almost Ripe; this has a pent house over it which is cover'd up very Close in the winter.

Here are some of her observations on food. Coarse fish was eaten by seventeenth-century Englishmen.

> In this parke [she writes], is severall ponds wch affords good ffish, as does ye moate and ye Trent, as trout, Eeles, tench, perch, etc., the largest perch I ever saw just Caught and dress'd immediately wch Eates in perfection.
>
> Charr ffish . . . wch they pott with sweete spices. They are as big as a small trout, Rather slenderer and ye skinn full of spotts, some Red Like the finns of a Perch and the inside flesh Looks as Red as any salmon if they are in season; their taste is very rich and fatt tho' not so strong or Clogging as the Lamprys.

In Westmorland, Celia saw oat clap bread being made:

> They mix their flour with water, so soft as to rowle it in their hands into a ball, and then they have a board made round and something hollow in the middle; [the dough was clapped into this, and then] drive it to ye Edge in a Due proportion till drove as thinn as a paper and still they Clap it and drive it round, and then they have a plaite of iron same size with their Clap board, and so shove off the Cake on it and so set it on Coales and bake it; when Enough on one side they slide it off and put the other side . . . they have no other sort of bread unless at market towns.

This sounds good. In Cornwall she ate West-Country tart, which was an

> apple pye with a Custard all on the top, its ye most acceptable entertainment it Could be made me. They scald their creame and milk in most parts of those Countrys, and so its a sort of Clouted Creame as we Call it, with a Little sugar and soe put on ye top of ye apple Pye. I was much pleased with my supper tho' not with the Custome of the Country wch is a universal smoaking, both men, women, and children have all their pipes of tobacco in their mouths and soe sit round the fire smoaking.

She gives an odd recipe for manufacturing soap. The makers burnt fern or bracken and then took the ashes "wch they make fine and Rowle them up in Balls and so sell them or use them all ye year for washing and scouring, and send much up to London".

Celia went to Tunbridge Wells to drink the water; and she

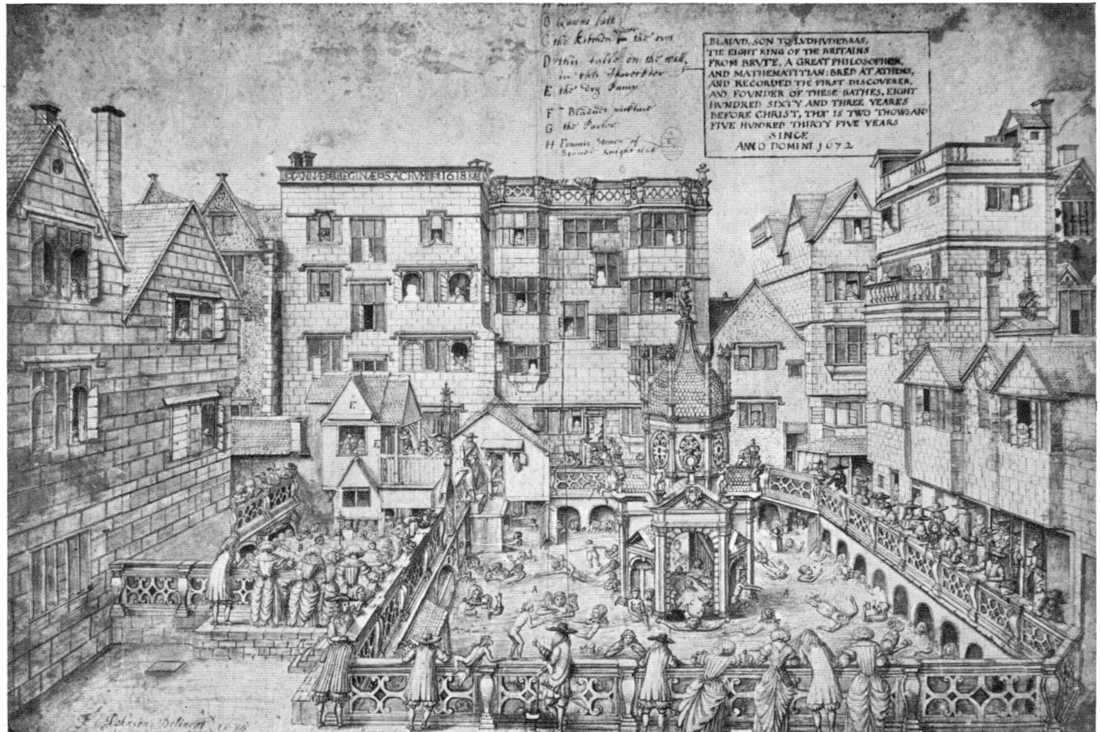

85 The Baths at Bath, 1675

From a Contemporary Drawing by P. Johnson in the British Museum

bathed at Bath. There was a cross, she tells us, in the middle of one bath with seats round it for gentlemen; and round the wall were arches with seats for the ladies, with curtains in front. They all sat up to their necks in the water. There was a gallery round the top from which idlers could view the proceedings. In the King's bath the water was hotter, and you could have it pumped over you; in which case you wore a broad-brimmed hat. The ladies bathing donned garments, made large with great sleeves like a parson's gown, of a fine, stiff yellow canvas—"the water fills it up so that its borne off that your shape is not seen". The gentlemen had drawers and waistcoats of the same material. To go out of the baths, the ladies passed within a door and went up steps and let their canvas bathing clothes slip off; meanwhile their maids put

> a garment of flannell made like a Nightgown with great sleeves over your head, and ye guides take ye taile and so pulls it on you Just as you rise ye steps, and yr other garment drops off so you are wrapped up in ye flannel and your nightgown on ye top, and your slippers, and so you are set in chaire which is brought into ye roome. . . . Ye chaires you go in are a low seate and with frames round and over yr head and all cover'd inside and out with red bayes and a Curtaine drawn before of ye same wch make it Close and warme; then a couple of men with staves takes and carryes you to your lodging and sets you at yr bedside where you go to bed and lye and sweate some tyme as you please.

Fig. 85, taken from a fine contemporary drawing in the British Museum, made a few years before Celia's visit, gives a graphic impression of the scene.

There are constant references in Celia's diary to the badness of the roads. The hard high roads of the Romans, on which the Legions had marched, were so neglected that Watling Street is described as being "deep heavy ground". Again, near Leicester she encountered "very deep bad roads . . . I was neer 11 hours going but 25 mile". Celia mentions that in Lancashire "they have one good thing . . . that at all Cross wayes there are posts with hands pointing to each road with ye names of ye great town or market towns that it Leads to". This was not general, for in Derbyshire Celia had to hire guides. Ordinary folk could not help you, because they did not know the country more than two or three miles from their own homes.

Where the roads were so bad, pack-horses (95) were used for the trade and industry, which was still very primitive but beginning to develop. Here is the description of a coal-mine at Chesterfield in Derbyshire:

> They make their mines at ye Entrance Like a Well and so till they Come to ye Coale then they digg all the Ground about where there is Coale and set pillars to support it, and so bring it to ye well where by a basket Like a hand barrow by Cords they pull it up—so they Let down and up the miners with a Cord.

Kent and Sussex were still the Black Countries; and the iron-ore found there was smelted with charcoal. There, as Celia says,

> when they have lighted ye fire for to Cast bells or guns they must be Cautiously blowing, and ye mettle will be apt to fall down on the nose of ye bellows and harden; that if it be not still Cleared off, would quickly damn up the fire and put it out.

Perhaps this trade led to the old proverb that "A yeoman of Kent with one year's rent Could buy out ye Gentleman of Wales and knight of Sscales and a Lord of ye North Country."

Celia tells us how tin was mined in Cornwall. Fine flowered silks were woven in Canterbury; crapes, calamanco, and damasks in Norwich; serges in Exeter; stockings in Nottingham; paper in Kent; baize at Colchester.

The manufacture of serge at Exeter she describes as follows: The yarn was spun by the spinners, who brought it to market and sold it to the weavers, who wove it on their own looms. They sold the woven serge to the fullers, who put it into the fulling mills. Here it was turned round and about by "huge notched timbers like great teeth" in vats of a mud made of fuller's earth, to remove the oil and grease.

> When they are thus scour'd they drye them in racks strained out wch are as thick set one by another as will permitt ye dresser to pass between, and huge large fields occupy'd this way almost all the round the town wch is to the river side.

The knots were then picked out, and the serge folded, with a paper between each fold, and put in a screw-press, which had a coal fire on the top plate. Some serges were dyed, but those for London were white. This gives an excellent idea of how

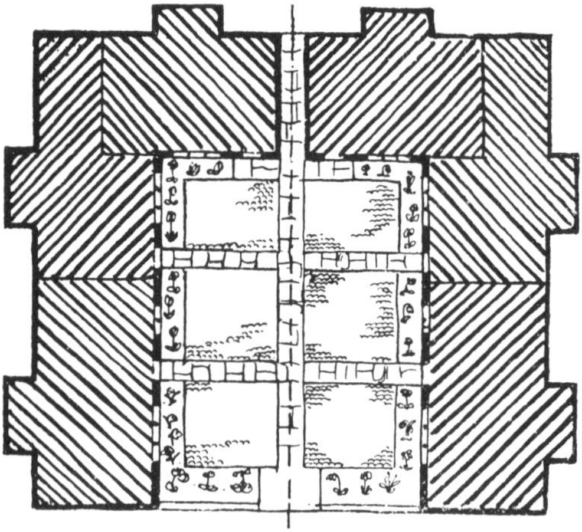

86 Plan of Almshouses at Amersham (87, 88)

manufacture was carried on by a number of artisans, each working in his own workshop.

Figs. 87 and 88 show a very pleasant group of almshouses at Amersham, Buckinghamshire, built by Sir William Drake during the Commonwealth. We do not know whether Celia saw them in her travels; but, if she did, we expect she would have considered the design rather old-fashioned. The flavour of Tudor times remains in the shape of the arch windows, and doors, and the gabled ends. Celia preferred a more full-blooded Renaissance treatment. At the Dissolution of the Monasteries, many poor people, who had looked to the monks for support, were left stranded; so it became the fashion for pious people to build almshouses where the poor could find a refuge. There was something about the idea that stimulated architects, for almshouses seem always to have been treated very successfully. Fig. 86 shows how the six cottages at Amersham were planned round the entrance to the courtyard.

MUSICIANS AND THEIR INSTRUMENTS

We have described how Willen Church expresses the seventeenth-century character of its founders; and the same parallel could be drawn between architecture and music. When architecture tends to decorative complication, music is apt to follow suit; and both help to convey the spirit of their period.

Fig. 89 gives Dido's Lament, "When I am laid in earth", from *Dido and Æneas*, by Henry Purcell, 1658–95, as a typical seventeenth-century song.

A great deal of care was devoted to the design of musical

The Courtyard

87, 88 The Almshouses at Amersham, Buckinghamshire
Built by Sir William Drake, 1657

89 "When I am laid in Earth." Dido's Lament
By Henry Purcell, 1658–95

90 A Spinet, end of Seventeenth Century

instruments. Fig. 90 shows a spinet, or virginal, of the end of the seventeenth century. We see here the next improvement on the clavicytherium of the sixteenth century. As this instrument has been laid flat on its back, the family relationship with the harp is not so easy to trace. Played from a keyboard, the keys are balanced levers, having at the far end a jack, to which is attached a metal point, leather spine, or a quill, which plucks the strings as the jack is pressed up by the key. The spinet shown is separate from the stand on which it is placed. Describing the Great Fire of 1666, Pepys writes of seeing the Thames "full of lighters and boats taking in goods, and I observed that hardly one lighter or boat in three, that had the goods of a house in, but there was a pair of virginalls in it."

Fig. 91 illustrates a gentleman playing a recorder with great content. This was a whistle flute, or flageolet. "Being returned home," recorded Pepys, again in the year of the Great Fire, "I find Greeting, the flageolet-master, come, and teaching my wife; and I do think my wife will take pleasure in it, and it will be easy for her, and pleasant." Pepys was very fond of music. He writes of "my dear Mrs. Knipp, with whom I sang, and in perfect pleasure I was to hear her sing, and especially her little Scotch song of Barbary Allen". And here is a pretty picture, which reminds us that the Thames in his day was a more agreeable stream than it is now, and more often used by Londoners: ". . . so to the Cherry Garden, and then by water singing finely to the Bridge, and there landed".

91 A Recorder, 1683

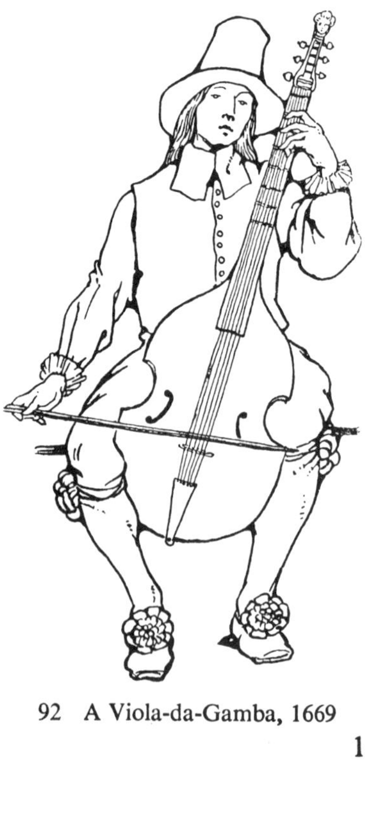

92 A Viola-da-Gamba, 1669

KITCHENS AND DINING-ROOMS

A great deal of information can be gathered from Pepys as to the sort of food that people ate in Charles II's reign. On January 1st, 1660, the diarist "Dined at home in the garret, where my wife dressed the remains of a turkey, and in the doing of it she burnt her hand." But they went out to dinner on January 6th: "only the venison pasty was palpable mutton, which was not handsome". On June 10th, 1663, they went "to the whay-house and drank a good deal of whay". September 8th, 1663, "being washing-day, we had good pie baked of a leg of mutton". At a banquet, "many were the tables, but none in the Hall but the Mayor's and the Lords of the Privy Council that had napkins or knives, which was very strange". On March 10th, 1664: "To dinner with my wife to a good hog's harslet [from pig's inside], a piece of meat I love." On June 15th, 1664: "Very merry we were with our pasty very well baked; and a good dish of roasted chickens, pease, lobsters, strawberries." Later on, "Come W. Bowyer, and dined with us; but strange to see how he could not endure onyons in sauce to lamb . . . and so was forced to make his dinner of an egg or two." "Hare pye" is said to be "very good meat", and fritters are mentioned on a Shrove Tuesday. Pepys and his family ate asparagus; on April 20th, 1667, the diarist went "home, having brought with me from Fenchurch Street a hundred of sparrow grass, cost 18*d*. We had them and a little bit of salmon . . . cost 3*s*."

The diary of John Evelyn gives us an account of a great feast given by Charles II, at the Banqueting-house at Whitehall, to "all the Companions of the Order of the Garter". He describes it thus:

> The King sat on an elevated throne at the upper end at a table alone; the Knights at a table on the right-hand, reaching all the length of the room; over against them a cupboard of rich gilded plate; at the lower end, the music; on the balusters above, wind-music, trumpets, and kettle-drums. The King was served by the lords and pensioners, who brought up the dishes. About the middle of the dinner, the Knights drank the King's health, then the King theirs, when the trumpets and music played and sounded, and the guns going off at the Tower. At the Banquet came in the Queen, and stood by the King's left hand, but did not sit. Then was the banqueting-stuff flung about the room profusely. In truth, the crowd was so great, that though I stayed all the supper the day before, I now stayed no longer than this sport began, for fear of disorder. The cheer was extraordinary, each Knight having forty dishes to his mess, piled up five or six high; the room hung with the richest tapestry.

Food was roasted, baked, or broiled; for the former an open fire would have been used, though coal was beginning to be burnt, probably in a long iron grate, or fire basket built of iron bars. Before this would have stood the fire-dogs, or andirons, with attachments in which the spits could turn. The joints and poultry were trussed on to these spits; there was a shallow tray beneath to take the drippings from basting; and the dripping we now eat on bread, or hot toast, is so called because it did at one time drip into the pan. The spits were sometimes turned by a clever mechanical arrangement such as is illustrated in fig. 93. This remarkable piece of smith's work dates from 1684. It was fixed on the outside of the chimney; and the spindle 5 went through the wall into the space at the side over the fire. The spindle 1 had a squared end on to which was fitted a loose handle; this turned round a wooden drum 2, independently of 4, and wound up a heavy weight. When the winding was completed, the action was reversed; and, by an ingenious stop, the drum at 2 turned the cogged-wheel 4 in an anti-clockwise direction; this engaged with 6, which was connected by a spindle to the prettily pierced wheel in front, the cogs of which were cut on the bevel to engage with the worm on spindle 8. The latter had a small fly-wheel fitted at 9 which acted as a governor. At the end of spindle 5 was a wooden pulley, from which lines were taken to wheels on the ends of the spits underneath; this acted like belting in a modern factory, and the spits were turned round

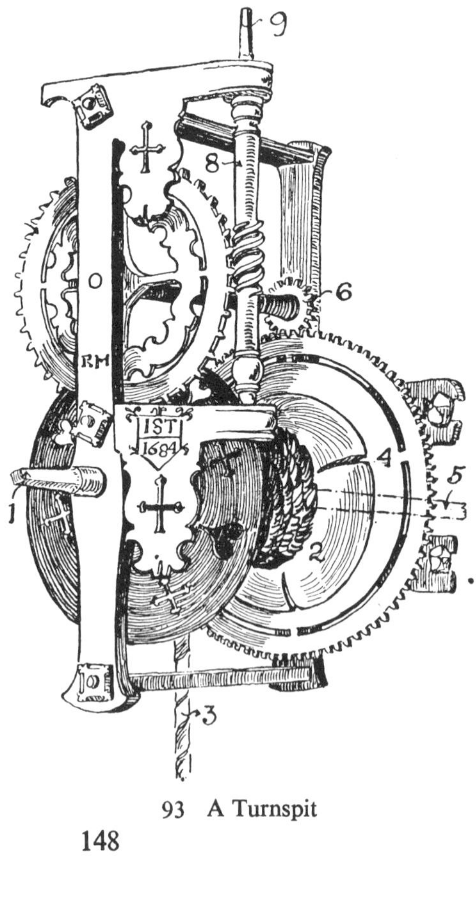

93 A Turnspit

and round. Pots were suspended over the fire by cranes, one of which is shown in fig. 152.

The baking was still done in a brick oven, in the way described in Vol. I, Chapter III. It is also usual to find in old kitchens that provision was made for cooking by charcoal. A sort of brick table was built up, with arches under it in which the charcoal was kept; and on the table little fires were built with this fuel, enclosed in metal rings, over which cooking was done in small pots.

Pepys was always trying to improve his house and make it look more attractive. As he became more prosperous, he bought a good deal of silver, some of it for use on the table. On September 9th, 1664, he writes: "I out and bought some things: among others, a dozen of silver salts . . . I this day putting my two flaggons upon my table. . . ." Later in the year, Pepys pays "the silver smith £22 18*s*. for spoons, forks, and sugar-box". On February 2nd, 1666: "Did carry home a silver drudger [to contain *dragées*, or sugar plums] for my cupboard of plate, and did call for my silver chafing-dishes." "Drinking glasses, a case of knives and other things" were bought later in the year; and, on December 31st, the diarist tells us with great satisfaction:

> One thing I reckon remarkable in my own condition is, that I am come to abound in good plate, so as at all entertainments to be served wholly with silver plates, having two dozen and a half.

Pepys's Diary is interesting because of the little human touches that make the characters in it live; and the diarist gives us not only the noble thoughts suitable for publication, but some of the mean ones too. It is interesting to watch his career; and, in the end, we follow his fortune with real affection. In 1660, Mr. and Mrs. Pepys had only one maid, Jane; but at the end of 1663, Jane, whose surname was Gentleman, had "Besse, our excellent good-natured cook-maid, and Susan, a little girl" to keep her company. By September 1664 the household had been increased, and we are told: "Up, and to church in the best manner I have gone a good while—that is to say, with my wife, and her woman, Mercer, along with us, and Tom, my boy, waiting on us." Pepys was a kindly man, but did not hesitate to punish his servants if need be. On February 19th, 1665, we are told: "I fell mightily out, and made my wife . . . to beat our little girle, and then we shut her doune into the cellar, and there she lay all night." Another time:

> Coming home, saw my door and hatch open, left so by Luce our cookmaid, which so vexed me, that I did give her a kick in our entry, and offered a blow at her, and was seen doing so by Sir W. Pen's footboy, which did vex me to the heart, because I know he will be telling their family of it.

Certainly the old ruffian deserved to feel ashamed of himself. But all the maids would not put up with this. In 1666 there was one of whom Pepys wrote:

> Up, and away goes Alice, our cookmaid, a good servant, whom we loved and did well by her, and she an excellent servant, but would not bear being told of any fault in the fewest and kindest words, and would go away of her own accord, after having given her mistress warning fickly.

Pepys and his wife give us, as we have seen, a very clear and illuminating picture of life in the mid-seventeenth century; and, as we read, we come to the conclusion that English home-management changed very little through the ages—at least until the end of Queen Victoria's reign, when women were still expected to attend to the smallest details of household affairs. Our grandmothers, we know, filled large books with treasured recipes, passed down from mother to daughter or given as a great favour by some friend. Many of the recipes recorded in *Pepys's Diary* are already known to us; but those of the wife of Oliver Cromwell are less familiar. In the British Museum is a small book written after the death of Cromwell, containing an account of his wife and his household, and the fashion of management therein. The book has been written in a vein of somewhat malicious gossip, to expose the frugality and even parsimony of the household; but, curiously enough, the impression it produces is that of a shrewd, sensible woman, who ruled her house wisely and well. The book speaks with horror of the herd of cows grazed in St. James's Park, although we are also led to believe that the resultant butter was excellent. Two of the recipes from her cooking book given here, and spoken of disparagingly as frugal and plain, appear far too rich for an ordinary modern meal:

TO MAKE GOOSEBERRY CREAM

First boyl, or you may preserve your Gooseberries, then having a clear Cream boyled up and seasoned with old Cinamon, Nutmeg, Mace, Sugar, Rose-water and Eggs, dish it up, and when it is cold take up the Gooseberries with a pin, and stick them in on rounds as thick as they can lye upon the said Cream, garnishing your Dish with them, and strow them over with the finest Sugar and serve them up.

TO BROYL OYSTERS

Take the biggest Oysters you can get, then take a little minced tyme, grated nutmeg, and grated bread, and a little salt, put this to the Oysters, then get some of the largest bottom shells and place them on the gridiron, and put two or three Oysters in each shell, then put some butter to them, and let them simmer on the fire till the liquor boils low, supplying it still with butter, when they are crisp feed them with white wine, and a little of their own liquor, with a little grated bread, nutmeg and minced tyme, but as much only as to relish it, so let it boyle up again, then add some drawn butter to thicken them, and dish them on a dish or plate, but if you have scollop shells it is the best way to broyl them in.

COACHES, CHARIOTS AND WAGONS

There was a great development in coachbuilding during the seventeenth century; and the Company of the Coach and Coach-Harness Makers was founded by Charles II in 1677. This points to improved roads and an increase in travelling. In Thrupp's *History of Coaches*, a very reasonable suggestion is made, that the coach invented at Kotze, in Hungary, in the fifteenth century was modelled on the German wagon, a sketch of which is given(94). This very much resembles the English timber wagon of today. 1 is the front axle-tree bed, and 2 the futchels which go through it. The pole at 4 is connected to the front of the futchels, and has the drawing-bars attached to it. 3 is the sway-bar fixed on the ends of the futchels, and arranged to work under the perch 7. 6 is the transom, which is pivoted on the axle-tree bed under it. The perch 7 is securely fixed into transom 6. As the wagon turns; the horses pull pole 4 round, which by futchels 2 turn axle-tree bed 1 under transom 6, and the sway-bar 3 moves under perch 7. 8 is the back axle-tree bed, and the perch fixes into this, or, as in the case of the timber

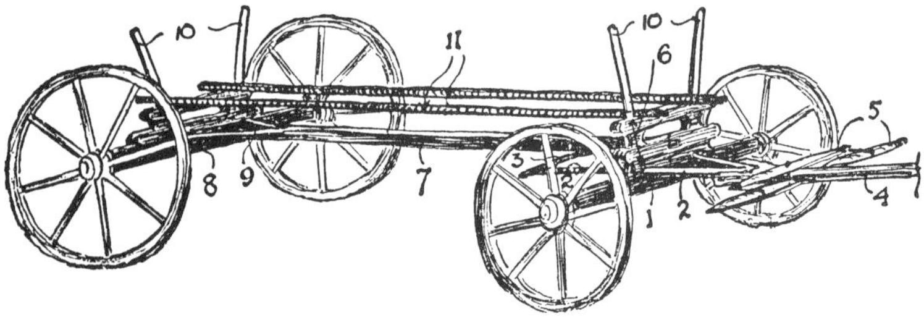

94 A German Wagon

wagon, slides through it; the wings at 9 give greater security. This explains why the front wheels of a wagon are smaller than those in the rear; they must be if the builder aims at a level perch. Standards at 10 were fixed into the transoms, and fir poles at 11 rested in between. Planks laid on these, and at the sides against the standards, made a very useful wagon. Mr. Thrupp thought the early coachbuilders made a start by doing away with the poles at 11, and after strengthening the standards 10, using them to suspend the body of the coach by means of leather braces. Certainly the latter were the first attempt at springing.

Fig. 97 shows a coach of the time of Charles II suspended in this way. The body was framed up in wood, covered with leather and studded with nails, and the roof is prettily domed. There are not yet any windows, and the door is a leathern curtain hanging from a movable iron bar. The body of the coach is not unlike that of the sixteenth century (55); but whereas the latter was mounted rather like a box on wheels, the seventeenth-century coach is a far more thoughtful production.

Fig. 99 shows a chariot such as Pepys might have selected. Chariots were smaller and lighter than coaches. Pepys tells us in his diary, on November 5th, 1668, how he went to see his coachmaker, and "did pitch upon a little chariott, whose body was framed, but not covered, it being very light, and will be very genteel and sober". In December he was "abroad with my wife, the first time that I ever rode in my own coach". The following April Pepys was "calling about my coach which hath been to the Coach-maker's to be painted and the window frames gilt again". So by this time coaches had windows. A few days later he found

95 A Pack Train

96 A Stage-wagon

97 A Coach and Four
From Engravings by D. Loggan, 1675

98 Stage-wagon, showing Passengers
From a Drawing by T. Rowlandson

TRANSPORT, LATE SEVENTEENTH AND EIGHTEENTH CENTURIES

> my coach is silvered over, but no varnish yet laid. I stood by it till eight at night, and saw the painters varnish it, and it dries almost as fast as it can be laid on. I sent the same night my coach-man and horses to fetch the coach home.

And the next day was May Day; so Pepys went "at noon to dinner, and after through the town with our new liveries of serge, and the horses' manes and tails tied up with red ribbons, and new green rains"; and doubtless our old friend was very pleased with his gay turn-out.

In 1605 we learn that "coaches have increased with a mischief, and have ruined the trade of the waterman by hackney coaches, and now multiply more than ever". Another reminder of how much the Thames was used for communication is to be found in *Evelyn's Diary*:

> I was spectator of the most magnificent triumph that ever floated on the Thames, considering the innumerable boats and vessels, dressed and adorned with all imaginable pomp, but, above all the thrones, arches, pageants, and other representations, stately barges of the Lord Mayor and Companies, with various inventions, music, and peals of ordnance, both from the vessels and the shore, going to meet and conduct the new Queen from Hampton Court to Whitehall, at the first time of her coming to town. In my opinion it far exceeded all the Venetian Bucentoras, etc., on the Ascension, when they go to espouse the Adriatic.

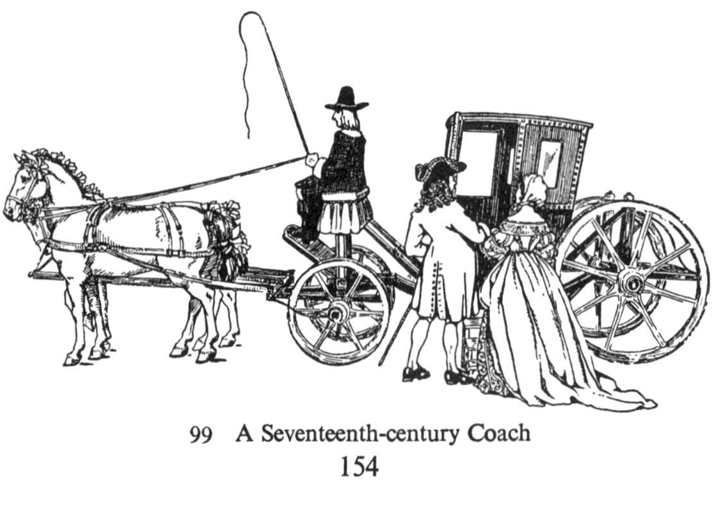

99 A Seventeenth-century Coach

> His Majesty and the Queen came in an antique-shaped open vessel, covered with a state or canopy, of cloth of gold, made in form of a cupola, supported with high Corinthian pillars, wreathed with flowers, festtoons, and garlands. I was in our new-built vessel sailing amongst them.

Sedan-chairs (139) were in use in 1634, and Pepys writes in 1667 of "Sir John Winter, poor man! come in a sedan from the other end of the town."

Berlins were invented in 1660 at Berlin. They had two perches instead of one; and between these, from the front transom to the back axle-tree, two strong leather braces were stretched, going right under the coach body, and made adjustable by small windlasses, so that they could be slackened or tightened as desired. Experiments were made about this time in the use of springs.

As early as the end of the sixteenth century, long broad-wheeled wagons (98) travelled between towns with goods and passengers, and were called "stages". Stage-coaches began to run about 1640, and resembled large private coaches. Outside passengers sat in a basket between the hind wheels, as shown in Hogarth's picture of "The Inn Yard" painted in 1730.

LIBRARIES AND MUSEUMS

Fig. 100 is of a library, dating from 1675, designed by Sir Christopher Wren for Trinity College, Cambridge. In Vol. I, Chapter IV, a library was shown in which the books were chained to desks like long church lecterns, with a shelf underneath for the storage of additional volumes; but this belongs to the days before printing, when books were all hand-made, and precious and scarce. When Caxton began work at Westminster in 1476, it was possible to bring out an edition of several books, instead of one at a time as before—an innovation that had its effect on storage. More shelves were added to the lecterns; the arrangement was that of a double set of bookshelves, back to back, with desks under them. Examples can be seen at Corpus Christi College, Oxford (1517), and Merton College, Oxford; but for a long time books were still chained to the shelf. Cases were placed down the room at right angles to the walls; and there was generally a window at ordinary height between each set of cases, and a seat or bench. This is called the stall system, because stalls or compartments are formed between the cases.

100 A Seventeenth-century Library
Trinity College, Cambridge, by Wren

The library at Durham Cathedral is a late example of the type, and dates from the end of the seventeenth century; but shortly afterwards, when chaining was done away with, students ceased to need the desk as a book-rest. Peterhouse, Cambridge, 1641–8, and University Library, Cambridge, 1649–50, omitted it, and reached the limit of development possible in the stall system.

Wall cases had been set up in the Bodleian in 1612; and Wren combined them with stall cases, and raised his windows so that the two could range. He described his work in this way:

> The disposition of the shelves, both along the walls and breaking out from the walls, must needes prove very convenient and gracefull, and the best way for the students will be to have a little square table in each celle with 2 chairs.

Wren designed table, book-rest, and stools. The bookcases were panelled up in oak, and enlivened with carving in lime by Grinling Gibbons. The oblong panels in the ends are door fronts to small catalogue cupboards. In the library at St. Paul's, Wren used wall cases with a delightful little gallery around to reach the higher shelves.

In the Pepysian Library, Magdalene College, Cambridge, are the bookcases that Pepys caused to be constructed for his own use. "Comes Simpson, the joyner," he wrote in 1666, "and he and I with great pains contriving presses to put my books up in"; and a little later: "Much pleased to-day with thoughts of gilding the backs of all my books alike, in all my new presses."

With this great new interest in books, we reach another stage in the development of our civilisation. We notice the emergence of the scientific spirit. In 1645 the nucleus of what was to become a very great society was formed. This consisted of a band of men who met together to discuss the new, or experimental, Philosophy. The seeds of the movement had already been sown by Leonardo da Vinci, Giordano Bruno, Galileo, and Francis Bacon; and it flowered in the Royal Society founded in 1660.

From 1680 to 1682 Sir Christopher Wren was president, and the business of the meetings consisted of discussions of natural phenomena and the display of scientific experiments. One paper, for example, was read to prove that "small fossils be the result of the deluge", though Dr. Martin Lister contended in reply tnat they were "separate organisms fashioned on their own". Yet another member, a one-time president of the Society, read a paper to prove that "barnacles turned into birds". From such modest beginnings the Society moved slowly forward, until in the eighteenth century its membership broke into two sections—those who were true scientists and those who became merely collectors of curiosities. By the middle of the century the collection of the latter had become a fashionable pastime. To house collections of "curiosities", Slater's and Tradescant's museums were formed. The second was bequeathed by the younger Tradescant to Thomas Ashmole, who in turn bequeathed it in 1682 to the University of Oxford, and it became known as the Ashmolean Museum. The Tradescants were a remarkable botanical family who travelled far in search of rare plants. You can see a painting of a group in the Ashmolean galleries, and should visit their curious tomb in Lambeth churchyard. Fig. 118 shows a scientist in his study carrying out research on instruments of navigation.

SMELTING AND IRONWORK

The seventeenth-century architects thoroughly appreciated smith-craft; and, as there are several illustrations of ironwork in this part of our book, we propose to give a few details of early methods of ironworking. Iron is found in many parts of England, but is most valuable nowadays when it can be mined with the coal which is used to smelt it, as in Yorkshire, Derbyshire, and Staffordshire. In the old days, before coal was used, the Weald of Sussex was England's Black Country, and charcoal was used for smelting. The early workings were shallow, and abandoned as soon as the surface was worked out. The ore is found in many forms: at a remote period it may have been deposited by water, in a form now described as sedimentary rock, being in reality rather like accumulated rust. The early process of smelting was a very simple one. A furnace was built up, and first a layer of charcoal was put in, then another of iron ore, and then one of fuel, and so on. The blast was applied by bellows in much the same way as to a smith's fire today—in fact, a rough wall built round the smith's fire would convert it into a replica of an early blast-furnace. A small quantity of malleable iron was produced in this way, which was hammered up into a "bloom". Such iron was very pure and soft, and lent itself readily to hammering on the smith's anvil; the fault of modern iron is that, being smelted by coal, it is impregnated with sulphur, and is more brittle and less ductile than the old metal. It is iron's capacity for assimilating other materials that makes it so useful to us; for instance, by adding carbon we turn it into steel, and enormously increase its strength. But to go back to our early smith—he had to forge all his work from the "bloom" and, to save him the trouble, trip-hammers seem to have been the next development. They were worked by water-wheels, and the ponds that stored the water are still called hammer ponds in Sussex. The wheel turned an axle, which had cams on it, rather like those on the camshaft of a motor engine which lift the valves. Obviously, if a large beam was pivoted at the centre, and had a heavy hammer attached at one end, it could be raised or depressed at the other by the action of cams. Fig. 154 shows such a trip-hammer at work; though the scene is a century later, the action is identical; and a friend tells us he has recently seen the device in operation in the Dolomites. This early application of power is a subject of the greatest interest; and we must not forget that, until the steam-engine came, the millwright was dependent on wind and water.

A seventeenth-century writer indicates that the "bloom" was refined by heating and hammering:

> This they take out [he writes], and giving it a few strokes with their sledges, they carry it to a great weight hammer, raised like wise by the motion of a water-wheel, where applying it dexterously to the blows, they presently beat it out into a thick short square. This they put into the finery again, and, heating it red hot, they work it out under the same hammer till it comes into the shape of a bar in the middle with two square knobs at the ends.

Cast iron was produced by so improving the furnaces that the metal was much more liquefied, and could be run off into moulds—a process that makes it much harder than malleable iron, but more brittle. Cast iron was not much used in these early days, except for cannon, shot and firebacks. The railings round St. Paul's, however, were manufactured in the seventeenth century.

Rolling-mills seem not to have started before the beginning of the eighteenth century. Nowadays the equivalent of a "bloom" is brought to rollers cut to the shape of the pattern to be rolled. The white-hot ingot is put in on one side, and rolled through, coming out on the other roughly shaped and, of course, longer. It is passed through the rollers, first from one side, and then the other, getting longer at each journey, until finally it has assumed the proper shape. Rolling-mills are necessarily big places; and, when hard at work, they suggest the nether regions. The white-hot ingots and the iron bars or girders, rushing along the floor as they come through the rollers in all states of red heat, steam, and smoke, and men toiling and sweating at their task, all build up an impressive picture. Thus are produced all the rolled steel joists, bars, angles, tees, and mouldings needed for everyday use, which need only to be cut off to length. Very different was the problem of the seventeenth-century smith; any bars that he bought would have been far too irregular for immediate use and would have needed forging to shape.

Yet, thanks to the wonderful dexterity with which they employed hammer, anvil and chisel, the old craftsmen were able to produce such pieces of work as we have illustrated.

Fig. 101 shows an espagnolette bolt dating from about the time of William and Mary, made for a pair of iron casement windows. The scroll end *A* is really joined on to the lever arm at *B*, and turns on *C*, raising a catch at *D*, which so releases *E*, a short lever turning an upright bolt fastened to the other leaf of casement by *F*. At top and bottom of *E* are hooks which fasten this leaf to the frame. *G* is a spring that keeps the catch *D* in position over *E*, and thus fastens the whole. The staircase of the same house is seen in fig. 83.

In the design of iron gates, railings, balconies and staircases the smiths of the later seventeenth century excelled; and the craft was transformed by Jean Tijou, probably a Huguenot refugee,

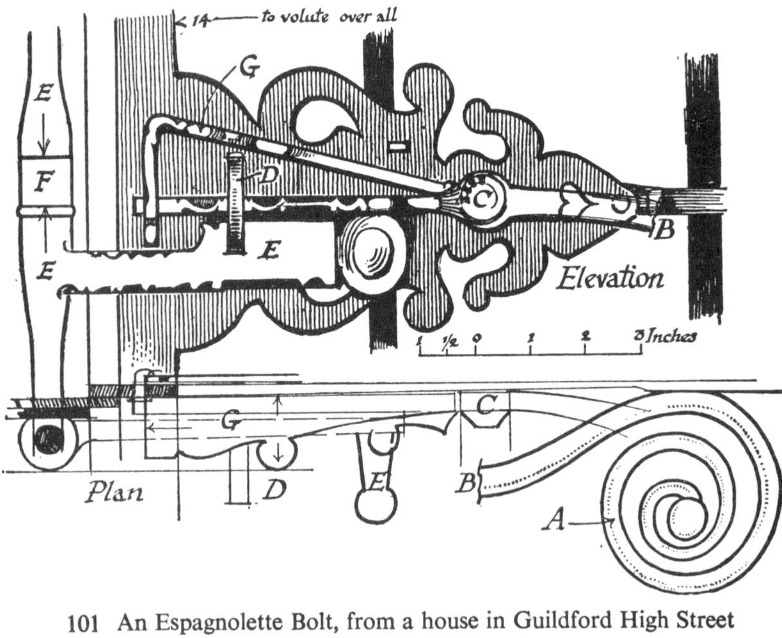

101 An Espagnolette Bolt, from a house in Guildford High Street

102 The Wheelwright

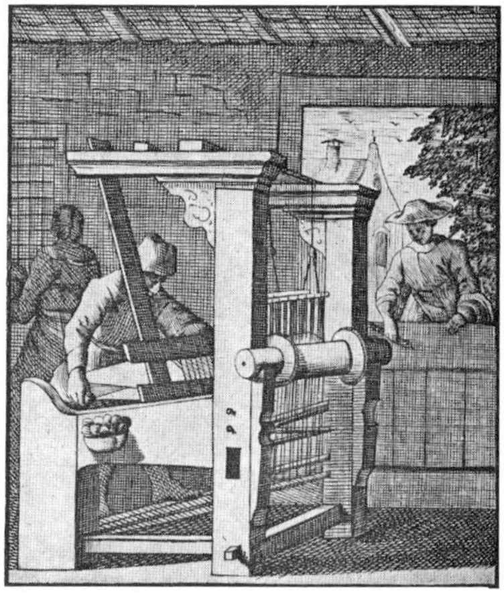

103 The Weaver

From a Late Seventeenth-century Book of Crafts

104 Interior of a Glassworks, showing furnace, with Glassblowing, and Pack-carriers setting out

105 Cresting or "Overthrow" of the "Golden Gates" of the Sanctuary, St. Paul's Cathedral
By Jean Tijou

whose work at Hampton Court and St. Paul's Cathedral should be studied for its glorious workmanship. An overthrow or cresting by Jean Tijou is shown in fig. 105. But one can derive almost as much pleasure from studying the simple effective ironwork in many English country towns. Other celebrated smiths were Bakewell of Derby, Edney of Bristol, and the brothers Roberts from Wales. The engraving of the first Eaton Hall(79) shows a magnificent curved forecourt screen by the brothers; its gates, altered and added to, still stand in the park.

We have already mentioned the establishment of the Vauxhall glassworks (p. 109); and fig. 104 takes us inside a glass factory of the time, with a furnace and blowers at work. There are several interesting books of trades published about 1680—those by Van Vliet, and the volume by Otten—where one sees workers making pottery or baskets, painting, printing, turning on the pole-lathe, and busily engaged in dozens of other crafts. We illustrate a weaver and a wheelwright in a carriage-builder's shop(102, 103).

SOLDIERING

Again we must turn to the arts of war. Figs. 106 and 107 show a pikeman and a musketeer of James I's reign. They are very similar to those of the Elizabethan period. The pikeman wears a helmet, breast- and back-plate, with tassets covering the thigh; and this equipment changed little until the reign of Charles II, when it was exchanged for a broad wideawake hat with feathers, and a long skirted coat. Pikemen were always used in conjunction with musketeers to protect the latter, when they were loading, against cavalry charges. For musketeers, when not actually firing, were an easy prey to the enemy—hopelessly cumbered with a heavy matchlock and rest, bandoliers, a powder-horn, a heavy pouch of bullets, a lighted rope match in their hands, and a sword girded at their side.

106 A Pikeman of James I's reign

In Charles II's reign a bayonet was invented that could be fixed on to the gun without stopping up the barrel; and this at once gave the musketeer a chance both of attacking and defending himself even when his gun was unloaded. Thenceforward the pike lost its principal function and gradually disappeared from warfare.

Cartridges were also introduced, containing the exact charge of powder and ball needed, which made loading a far speedier business and superseded the heavy pouches of bullets and dangerous bandoliers. These cartridges were cylinders of some strong material, each filled with a charge of powder and slung across one shoulder from a band.

Hand-grenades and small

explosive bombs came into use, and in *Evelyn's Diary* we read that in 1667

> I went to Greenwich where his Majesty was trying divers grenadoes shot out of canon at the Castlehill, from the house in the Park; they brake not till they hit the mark; the forged ones brake not at all, but the cast ones very well.

And again:

> Now were brought into service a new sort of soldiers, called Grenadiers, who were dexterous in flinging hand grenadoes, every one having a pouch full; they had furr caps with coped crowns like Janizaries, which made them look very fierce, and some had long hoods hanging down behind, as we picture fools. Their clothing being likewise piebald yellow and red.

An account of the dress of the new regiment formed by Charles II for the protection of his person, namely, the regiment of Life Guards, is interesting. It is thus described:

107 A Musketeer of James I's reign

> The privates wore round hats with broad brims, and a profusion of white feathers drooping over the hind part of the brim. They wore scarlet coats, richly ornamented with gold lace; sleeves wide, with a slash in front, and the lace lengthwise from the shoulder to the wrist; also white collars, which were very broad, and being turned over the vest, covered the neck, and spread over part of the shoulders. They wore scarlet sashes round the waist, tied behind, also large ruffles at the wrist, and long hair flowing over their

shoulders. Their boots were of jacked leather, and came up to the middle of the thigh. Their defensive armour were cuirasses and iron head-pieces called "potts"; their weapons, short carbines, pistols, swords, with a carbine belt suspended across the left shoulder. They rode long-tailed horses; on public occasions the tail was usually tied up, and together with the head and mane, decorated with a profusion of ribands.

108 An Officer of the Fifth Foot, 1688

This description is taken from *The Historical Records of Life Guards*; and it will be noticed that the dress corresponds very nearly with the horseman in fig. 62.

It was in the reign of Charles II that provision was made at Chelsea for old soldiers broken in the wars. The existing building, known as the Royal Hospital, was designed by Sir Christopher Wren, and owed its inspiration to Sir Stephen Fox, who was Paymaster of the Forces after the Restoration.

> Dined with Sir Stephen Fox [Evelyn records in his diary in 1681], who proposed to me the purchasing of Chelsea College, which his Majesty had sometime since given to our Society [the Royal Society], and would now purchase it again to build an hospital, or infirmary for soldiers there.

The wheel-lock was the next development in firearms, produced, no doubt, because the matchlock was so clumsy and difficult to use. One can almost imagine the musketeer with a matchlock, like an old-fashioned Victorian photographer, apologising to an enemy for being obliged to keep him waiting while he made his final preparations. It is saddening to think of all the time, energy, and good work spent in the world's history on the production of death-dealing instruments. So we leave the subject of war and turn to country life.

COUNTRY LIFE

After the restrictions of the Commonwealth, country sports and all kinds of hunting were followed with much zest and vigour. We have taken four subjects from Richard Blome's folio, *English Gentleman's Recreation* (1686), a grand old book, full of delightful engravings by Francis Barlow and I. Collins. Our quartet (109–10, 112–13) is composed of stag-, hare-, otter-hunting, and shooting—it looks decidedly odd to see the guns blazing away on horseback. In Blome's work fox-hunting, fishing with rod and net, and hawking for various birds, with accompanying dogs, are also illustrated. Hawking, however, was probably on the wane. Horse-races began to be regularly run during Charles II's reign, and Barlow has left us a lovely plate of the last race run before that king, near Windsor Castle.

A great deal of attention was given to agriculture in the seventeenth century; and, judging by the number of country houses built then, both large and small, it must have been in a prosperous condition. The open-field system, described in the last chapter, still existed side by side with farms which had been enclosed out of the demesne land. If the former was better for the labourer and cottager, the latter allowed the landlord and his tenant to adopt more progressive methods, and produce the surplus of food necessary for the increasing population of the towns. Enclosures caused much hardship; but ultimately they served a good purpose.

Good work was done at this time in draining the Fens; and we are apt to forget that much of this part of England in the seventeenth century was a waterlogged marsh inhabited mainly by wild-fowl. Gentlemen adventurers undertook the work of reclamation, for which they were to receive a large part of the land reclaimed. The Fenmen, being Englishmen, hated improvements on principle, and during the Civil War broke down the embankments, with a result that much of the land reverted to bog. A Dutchman, Sir Cornelius Vermuyden, was largely responsible for the direction of the works, and struggled to final success through years of heartbreaking disappointments. You can see one of the great straight 40-foot drains, stretching for miles over the flats, that is still known as "Vermuyden's Eau". With grim humour Cromwell sent him some thousands of Dutch naval prisoners.

> Being arrived at some meres [Evelyn notes in 1670], we found Lord Wotton, and Sir John Kiviet about their draining-engines, having, it seems, undertaken to do wonders, on a vast piece of

109 Otter-hunting
From an Engraving by F. Barlow

110 Shooting
From an Engraving by S. Gribelin

marsh-ground they had hired of Sir Thomas Chicheley. They much pleased themselves with the hopes of a rich harvest of hemp and coleseed, which was the crop expected.

Here we visited the engines and mills, both for wind and water, draining it through two rivers, or graffs, cut by hand, which went thwart one the other, discharging the water into the sea.

Evelyn was a great gardener, and wrote both on gardening and on farming. His book *Sylva* has interesting descriptions of early machinery; we read of a primitive type of saw-mill driven by a water-wheel, and a boring and shaping machine for making wooden drain-pipes.

In Worlidge's *Systema Agriculturae*, 1669, an illustration is given of a four-wheeled horse-drawn drill for sowing, which cut a furrow and sowed the seed in one operation, so that "one horse and man may work the instrument, and sow land as fast as, or faster than, six horses can plough".

Lord Sandwich presented Evelyn with a sembrador brought out of Spain—a wonderful engine, ploughing, sowing, and harrowing at once.

Another book, *England's Improvement*, was written by Captain Walter Blith about the time of Cromwell. He mentions the double-wheeled plough; the single-wheeled plough, and the foot-plough; the simple plain plough and a Dutch one, as being typical ones in use. We have reproduced his illustration in fig. 111. When one bears in mind how much the plough has meant to man, it is extraordinary how little attention has been paid to it.

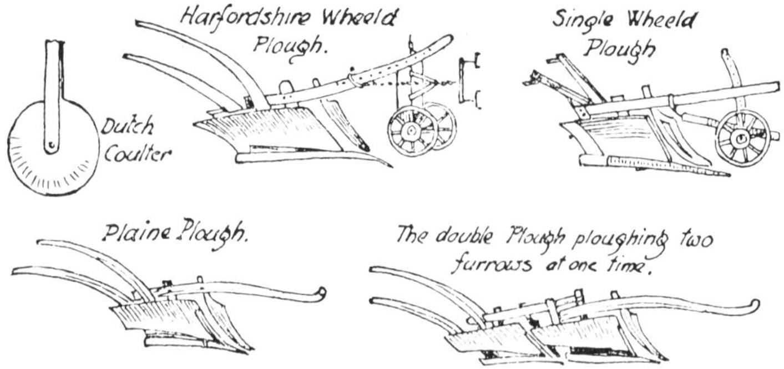

111 Ploughs From *England's Improvement*

112 Hare-hunting
From an Engraving by F. Barlow

113 Stag-hunting
From an Engraving by I. Collins

Writing of agriculture gives us the opportunity of illustrating the next important development in windmills. All the mills we have shown as yet have been of the post-mill variety, the whole mill balanced, and turning, on a central post. The one shown in fig. 114 is quite different. The old millers had probably begun to find that it was inconvenient to have to go about one's business in a moving workshop. It was essential, however, that the sails should turn to face the wind. This is how they overcame the difficulty. The octagonal body of the mill was constructed as a fixture below the head. The top of the octagon was finished with a circular curb, having strong wooden cogs projecting out of its circumference. The head, being framed up separately, was arranged to slide round on the top of the curb. The head and sails were turned into the wind by the little vane at the back. From the spindle of this vane a pair of bevel gears operated a vertical rod, which at its lower end had another pair of bevel gears; these turned a horizontal shaft with a worm cut on it, engaging with the cogs on the side of the curb. If the wind changed and the main sails went out of operation, the vane started to work, and the worm-gear, attached to the head of the mill, wormed its way along the cogs on the curb and turned the whole head round. When the main sails got into the wind again, the vane stopped. The chain hanging down operated an iron rod, which passed right through the centre of the main shaft and opened and shut the louvres on the sails—a really triumphant piece of work, to bore so long a hole by hand quite truly.

Millers had amusing names for the parts of a mill: the large cog wheel on the main shaft next to the sails is the brake wheel, and this engages with one called the wallowers. The one immediately under it, by means of gears, operates a sack hoist. The wheel under again is called the spur wheel, and this engages others called stone nuts, which turn the stones. The corn being hoisted up is emptied into the bins shown by dotted lines, and finds its way by gravity through shoots to the stones, and their slope can be adjusted to suit different grains. Peas, for instance, require a different angle to wheat.

The octagonal body is constructed of timber framing on a brick foundation; and, because the timber framing was covered with boarding and generally painted white, this type is called a smock mill. The little gallery around is a pretty feature; the old

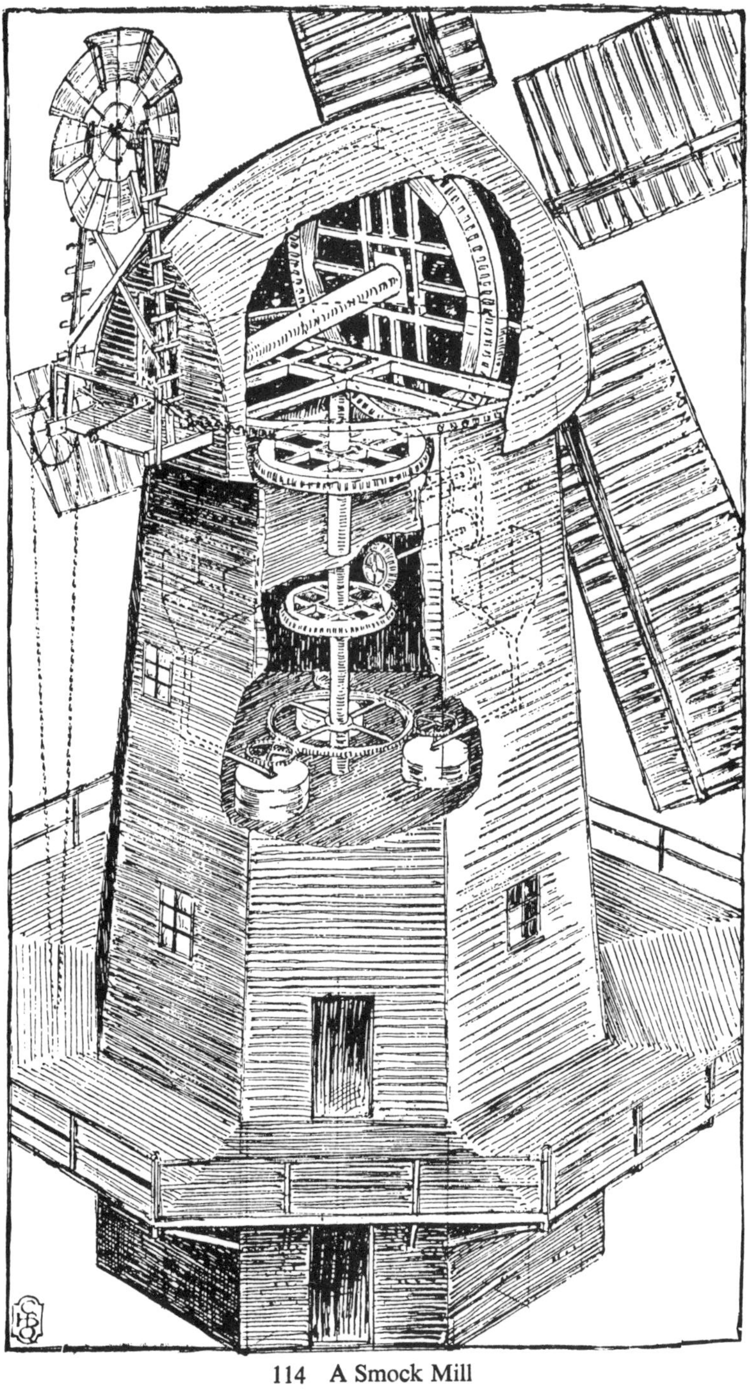

114 A Smock Mill

millwrights knew how to do their work, so that it formed a pleasant addition to the countryside.

THEATRES, DANCES, GAMES

At the beginning of the seventeenth century there were no great developments in theatre-building. When plague broke out, the theatres were closed for fear that they might help to spread the infection; and we hear of King James I authorising the "Boar's Head" and "Curtain" Theatres to reopen "as soon as the plague decreases to thirty deaths per week in London". In Charles I's time seven London playhouses were licensed—the Blackfriars Company, His Majesty's Servants, "The Bull", "Playhouse", "Fortune", "Globe", and "Cockpit", in Drury Lane. But during the Commonwealth they were all of them shut by the Puritan government except for the "Red Bull", which was allowed to give performances of "drolls", rope-dancing, etc.

At the Restoration a company of players started again at the "Red Bull", and eventually the old players reassembled and two companies were formed: one called themselves the King's House, and the other the Duke's Theatre. The "Duke's Theatre" in Little Lincoln's Inn Fields, opened in 1662, is thought to have been designed by Sir Christopher Wren. It was here that, for the first time after his Restoration, Charles II went to see a play. Compared with modern theatres, it was very small. Fig. 115 has been made from an old print; and it will be noticed that, although the design is much more modern than that shown in the sixteenth-century chapter, there are still points of resemblance. Over the proscenium are shown openings that may have been boxes, or have been put there in memory of the openings in the tower of the Elizabethan theatre, where the trumpeter was stationed to sound a note when the performance was starting. In the "Duke's Theatre" they were perhaps only painted representations, which afforded the decorator an opportunity to exercise his skill in perspective. Elaborate scenery was already beginning to be used; for example, a play was produced at the "Cockpit" entitled "*The Cruelty of the Spaniards in Peru,* expressed by vocal and instrumental music and by art of perspective in scenes."

Whereas, in the Elizabethan theatre, the pit was open to the sky, in the "Duke's Theatre" the body of the house appears to

115 A Seventeenth-century Theatre

have been covered in with a flat ceiling. But Pepys has a note in 1664: "To the King's House and saw 'The Silent Woman'. Before the play was done, it fell such a storm of hayle, that we in the middle of the pit were fain to rise; and all the house in a disorder." The "King's House" was a new theatre, built in Drury Lane, just after the "Duke's", which in all probability it resembled; and from this note of Pepys we can assume that the ceiling had a central open space. The print from which our drawing has been made shows only the margin ceiling just over the proscenium. For the rest of the interior of the "Duke's Theatre", the old print depicts three tiers of boxes as in the Elizabethan theatre, though the space on each side of the upper tier next to the stage (not being in a good position for seeing) has been used for decorative painting. The drawing shows a scene from Elkannah Settle's *Empress of Morocco.* Pepys has another description of theatre-going in 1667:

> . . . the stage is now . . . more glorious than heretofore. Now, wax-candles, and many of them; then, not above 3 lbs. of tallow; now, all things civil, no rudeness anywhere; then, as in a bear-garden: then, two or three fiddlers; now, nine or ten of the best: then, nothing but rushes upon the ground and everything else mean; now, all otherwise.

The Elizabethan theatre, indeed, had very closely resembled a bear-garden. Great changes for the better occurred during Pepys's lifetime.

The masque was very popular at the Court of James I, and his Queen, Anne, is supposed to have preferred masqueing to acting. Masques were spectacles rather than plays, and depended more on music, dancing, and transformation scenes than on plot. In the *Masque of Blackness*, given on Twelfth Night, 1606, the Queen and Court appeared with faces and arms blacked to represent Ethiopians; in the *Masque of Beauty*, an island was shown floating on water with beautiful effects of lighting. Inigo Jones the architect was employed to stage these performances, and made a great reputation by inventing the machinery that was necessary to effect the transformation scenes. Ben Jonson supplied the idea, and book of the words; and, alas! quarrelled with Jones, alleging that he obtained more than his fair share of credit. Jonson was a man of many parts. He started life as a bricklayer, served in the army in Flanders, and on his return became actor and playwright, probably at the "Curtain" in Shoreditch, and then with Henslowe at the "Rose" in Bankside. Here he quarrelled with another actor and, fighting a duel, killed his man. "Since you were with me," Henslowe wrote to Alleyne, "I have lost one of my company which hurteth me greatly, that is Gabriel, for he is slain in Hoxton Fields by the hands of Benjamin Jonson, bricklayer." Jonson in consequence found himself in gaol, and narrowly escaped hanging.

Jonson, of course, was one of the brilliant friends who used to meet Shakespeare at the "Mermaid Tavern". The "Devil Tavern" in Fleet Street was another of his haunts, and he also founded the Apollo Club, of which Herrick was a member. Jonson fell into poverty but, when he died, he was buried in Westminster Abbey, and on the stone Sir John Young paid a man 1*s.* 6*d.* to cut this brief epitaph: "O rare Ben Jonson".

Coffee was introduced about the middle of the century, and coffee-houses began to come into fashion as places of resort. "To the coffee-house [Miles's]," notes Pepys in 1660, "where were a great confluence of gentlemen; . . . where admirable discourse till 9 at night." Chocolate was advertised in 1657 as "an excellent West India Drink", and tea in 1658 as "China Drink".

Fig. 116 shows some of the mummers in a morris dance. This dance, which is believed to have originated in the East among the Moors, had certainly reached England as early as the fifteenth century, but seems especially characteristic of Elizabethan and Stuart times. Morris dances took place at weddings on Holy Thursday, and at the Whitsun Ales and Bride Ales; and a kind of pageant or play was also held, called *The Lord of Misrule.*

An amusing account is given by an Elizabethan writer of this ceremony. He tells how the Lord of Misrule is chosen by his fellows, how he is crowned, and then chooses others to be his bodyguard. Each follower wears a livery of yellow or green or some light colour; and they are bedecked with scarves, ribbons, laces, and gold rings and precious stones and jewels. On their legs are bands of either twenty or forty bells. They carry rich handkerchiefs in their hands or across their shoulders. The whole company includes drummers, pipers, dragons, hobby-horses, and other "antiques". They all march to the church:

116 A Morris Dance

> their pypers pypyng, their drummers thundering, their stumpes dauncing, their belles jyngling, their handkerchiefs fluttering about their heads like madde men, their hobbie horses and other monsters skirmishing amongst the throng, and in this sorte they goe to the church.

They dance into the church and out again, and finally feast in booths set up by the churchyard. The people around give them

> some bread, some good ale, some new cheese, some olde cheese, some custardes, some cracknels, some cakes, some flaunes, some tartes, some creame, some meat, some one thing and some another.

Thus they banquet and dance all day, and maybe all night too.

The characters in a morris dance varied. The most usual were Robin Hood, Little John, Friar Tuck, Maid Marian, the Queen of the May, the fool, the piper, and several other dancers, who very often included a hobby-horse and a dragon. Maid Marian was represented by a boy. The fool usually carried a ladle to hold alms, with a bladder attached, and a fox's brush on the tail of his tunic. Bells and handkerchiefs were always used.

In the churchwarden's accounts in Kingston is preserved a note of morris dancers' dress in the reign of Henry VIII. They were dressed in gilt leather and silver paper, and sometimes in coats of white-spangled fustian. They had purses at their

117 Costume of the Seventeenth Century

girdles, and garters with bells attached. Sometimes bells were jingled in the hand or fastened to the arms and wrists. Morris dancing continued until the end of the eighteenth century.

May Day was always kept as a holiday, with May Day games, morris dancing, and dancing round the maypole. Some say that the May Day revelry had its origin in the Roman "Floralia". The poems of Herrick contain many charming descriptions of how May Day was kept during the sixteen-forties. Thus in "Corinna's going a-Maying" he speaks of the custom of placing boughs of may over each door:

> Each Porch, each doore, ere this,
> An Arke a Tabernacle is
> Made up of white-thorn neatly enterwove;
> As if here were those cooler shades of love.

And again:

> A deale of Youth, ere this, is come
> Back, and with white-thorn laden home.
> Some have dispatcht their Cakes and Creame
> Before that we have left to dreame.

Candlemas Day, or the Feast of the Purification of the Virgin Mary, held on February 2nd, was usually marked by revelry; and in *Evelyn's Diary* he writes of the performance of a masque. Herrick refers to an odd superstition in connection with the eve of Candlemas:

> Down with the Rosemary, and so
> Down with the Baies, and Misletoe;
> Down with the Holly, Ivie, all,
> Wherewith ye drest the Christmas Hall:
>
> That so the superstitious find
> No one least Branch there left behind:
> For look, how many leaves there be
> Neglected there (maids trust to me)
> So many Goblins you shall see.

Fairs were still held; and Evelyn mentions both Bartholomew's Fair and Our Lady Fair at Southwark. At each of these he saw jugglers and performing animals. He also records having seen an Italian puppet-show in a booth at Charing Cross. He does not say if this was a Punch and Judy show; but Punch and Judy were undoubtedly introduced into England about this time, as were marionettes and dancing dolls. Jugglers, acrobats, fire-eaters, and other performers were often hired to entertain people at private houses after a dinner- or supper-party.

Here is Evelyn's picture of a professional fire-eater entertaining his audience:

> He devoured brimstone on glowing coals before us, chewing and swallowing them; he melted a beer-glass and eat it quite up; then, taking a live coal on his tongue, he put on it a raw oyster; the coal was blown with bellows till it flamed and sparkled in his mouth, and so remained till the oyster gaped and was quite boiled. Then he melted pitch and wax with sulphur, which he drank down, as it flamed; I saw't flaming in his mouth a good while; with divers other prodigious feats.

Billiards is mentioned in the diary, and skating too, skate blades having been introduced into England by Royalists returning from exile in Holland.

Children's games were much the same as in the Elizabethan era; but a new system of education was started by a German named Komensky, which corresponds very nearly to the Froebel Kindergarten system of today. He advocated that children should be taught through their play to make clay models, coloured mats and baskets with strips of bright paper, and that they should learn about various trades by means of action songs. Alphabetical bricks had been invented by Sir Hugh Platt in the reign of Elizabeth. Children's card-games are often spoken of, and we read that grammatical card-games were popular.

An interesting seventeenth-century engraving shows a primitive magic-lantern working; and it is described in a reference book of 1719 as

> a little optical machine which enables one to see in the dark, on a white wall, many spectres and frightful monsters of a sort that those who do not know the secret, believe it to be done by magic art.

Scientific instruments—thermometers and barometers—began to be manufactured by P. Pastonelli in Leather Lane, and fire-extinguishing engines in Cross Street in 1700.

A game called "Pale-maille" was played by men as well as

118 A Scientist investigating Navigation Instruments. Note the Typical Interior
From an Engraving by J. Stradanus

by children. It was not unlike golf, except that the ball, struck with a mallet or club, was driven through a hanging hoop. Charles II and his courtiers practised pale-maille in St. James's Park; and the walk in which they played has been called Pall Mall ever since.

SEVENTEENTH-CENTURY ORNAMENT

We conclude with our usual decorative tail-piece, which this time shows a characteristic example of Grinling Gibbons's carving. The great charm of Gibbons's work is that, although at first sight it seems to be a riot of exquisitely carved fruit and flowers, on closer inspection they appear to be woven into beautiful and harmonious designs. If this woodcarving is examined, it will be clear that the masses are carefully arranged and balanced, and that the lines of the cornucopia on each side, with the eagle over, supply a framework that unifies the whole and gives relief to the general richness. Without this design, the carving would be only a lovely confusion of natural forms.

Grinling Gibbons's fine craftsmanship can be seen in abundance at St. Paul's Cathedral—the choir-stalls, bishop's throne, and organ case—at St. James's, Piccadilly, and Hampton Court. Fine carving of a more architectural type is found in the London City churches. Perhaps the finest room in London was the vestry of St. Lawrence Jewry, destroyed in the Second World War, where the woodcarving of large swags was in oak, with a well-modelled high-relief plaster ceiling and, in the centre, a painting by an artist called Fuller.

119 Seventeenth-century Ornament

120 A Horseman of the Time of George II

Chapter III
EIGHTEENTH CENTURY

THE eighteenth century was a period of tremendous happenings. At home Great Britain was transformed from an agricultural into an industrial country; abroad, wars were waged that laid the foundation of the British Empire. But, though we gained vast possessions all over the globe, either by conquest or by discovery, across the Atlantic the American Colonists shook off their allegiance to the British Crown; and the original thirteen States proclaimed their independence in 1776. Both on the continent of Europe and beyond the seas, France remained our chief rival; and when, towards the end of the century, Napoleon arose to challenge us, only our sea-power—as in Elizabethan days—enabled us to hold our own.

Meanwhile, as our empire grew, British merchants and manufacturers prospered. Our trade overseas increased by leaps and bounds. England was soon to become the workshop of the modern world. The Industrial Revolution had already started;

Dates	Kings and Queens of England and France	Famous Men	Great Events	Principal Buildings
1702	Queen Anne, *m.* Prince George of Denmark	Duke of Marlborough *b.*	War with France	Castle Howard, Yorks., 1702–14
1703	. . . . . .	. . . . . .	. . . . . .	St. Catherine College Chapel, Cambridge
1704	. . . . . .	John Wood of Bath *b.*—A.	Battle of Blenheim. Capture of Gibraltar	
1705	. . . . . .	Francis Boucher *b.*—P.		
1706	. . . . . .	Benjamin Franklin *b.*	Battle of Ramillies	
1707	. . . . . .	Fielding *b.*—W.	Union between England and Scotland	
1708	. . . . . .	. . . . . .	Battle of Oudenarde	
1709	. . . . . .	Samuel Johnson *b.*—W.	Battle of Malplaquet	
1710	. . . . . .	. . . . . .	. . . . . .	St. Paul's Cathedral finished
1711	. . . . . .	Hume *b.*—W.	Archduke Charles made Emperor	
1713	. . . . . .	Sterne *b.*—W.	Treaty of Utrecht	Easton Neston, Northants.
1714	George I, *m.* Sophia Dorothea of Zell	Gluck *b.*—M.		
1715	. . . . . .	. . . . . .	. . . . . .	Blenheim Palace, Oxford
1716	*Louis XV of France*	Thomas Gray *b.*—Pt.		
1717	. . . . . .	David Garrick *b.* Horace Walpole *b.*—W.		St. Mary-le-Strand
1718	. . . . . .	Peg Woffington *b.*		
1720	. . . . . .	Rev. Gilbert White *b.*—W.	South Sea Bubble	Seaton Delaval, Northumberland
1721	. . . . . .	Smollett *b.*—W.		
1723	. . . . . .	Sir Joshua Reynolds *b.*—P.		Houghton, Norfolk
1725	. . . . . .	Greuze *b.*—P.		
1726	. . . . . .	James Wolfe *b.* Robert Adam *b.*—A.		St. Martin-in-the-Fields
1727	George II, *m.* Caroline of Brandenburg-Anspach	Gainsborough *b.*—P.		
1729	. . . . . .	Goldsmith *b.*—W.		
1731	. . . . . .	William Cowper *b.*—Pt.		
1732	. . . . . .	Haydn *b.*—M.		
1733	. . . . . .	. . . . . .	Excise Bill	
1734	. . . . . .	George Romney *b.*—P.		
1737	. . . . . .	. . . . . .	. . . . . .	Radcliffe Library, Oxford, 1737–47
1740	. . . . . .	James Boswell *b.*—W.		
1742	. . . . . .	. . . . . .	War of the Austrian Succession	Horse Guards, London
1743	. . . . . .	. . . . . .	Battle of Dettingen	
1745	. . . . . .	. . . . . .	Battle of Prestonpans	
1746	. . . . . .	. . . . . .	Battles of Falkirk and Culloden	
1747	. . . . . .	. . . . . .	. . . . . .	Woburn Abbey, Beds.
1748	. . . . . .	. . . . . .	Treaty of Aix-la-Chapelle	
1749	. . . . . .	Goethe *b.*—W. Edward Jenner *b.*		
1750	. . . . . .	Robert Clive		Prior Park, Bath
1751	. . . . . .	Sheridan *b.*—W.		
1752	. . . . . .	Chatterton *b.*—Pt. Frances Burney *b.*—W.		
1754	. . . . . .	William Pitt		Holkham Hall, Norfolk
1756	. . . . . .	Raeburn *b.*—P. Mozart *b.*—M.	Seven Years' War	
1757	. . . . . .	Kemble *b.* Blake *b.*—Pt.	Battle of Plassey	
1758	. . . . . .	Horatio Nelson *b.*		
1759	. . . . . .	John Hoppner *b.*—P. Robert Burns *b.*—Pt.	Capture of Quebec. Battle of Minden	
1760	George III, *m.* Charlotte of Mecklenburg-Strelitz			Harewood House, Yorks.
1761	. . . . . .	. . . . . .	. . . . . .	Kedleston, Derbyshire
1762	. . . . . .	Mrs. Jordan *b.*		
1763	. . . . . .	Morland *b.*—P.	Peace of Paris	
1768	. . . . . .	. . . . . .	. . . . . .	Adelphi Terrace
1769	. . . . . .	George Washington		
1770	. . . . . .	Beethoven *b.*—M. Wordsworth *b.*—Pt.	Ministry of Lord North and American War of Independence	
1771	. . . . . .	Warren Hastings. Sir Walter Scott *b.*—W.	Liberty of Press established	
1772	. . . . . .	Coleridge *b.*—Pt.		Ely House, Dover Street
1774	*Louis XVI of France*	Southey *b.*—Pt.		
1775	. . . . . .	Turner *b.*—P. Jane Austen *b.*—W. Charles Lamb *b.*—W. W. S. Landor *b.*—W.	Battles of Lexington and Bunker's Hill	
1776	. . . . . .	John Constable *b.*—P.	Declaration of Independence	Somerset House, Strand
1777	. . . . . .	. . . . . .	Surrender of Burgoyne at Saratoga	
1778	. . . . . .	. . . . . .	French Alliance with America	
1780	. . . . . .	Burke	Gordon Riots	
1782	. . . . . .	. . . . . .	. . . . . .	Newgate Prison
1783	. . . . . .	William Pitt the younger	Treaty of Versailles	
1784	. . . . . .	Leigh Hunt *b.*—Pt.		
1785	. . . . . .	Thomas de Quincey *b.*—W.		
1787	. . . . . .	Edmund Kean *b.*		
1788	. . . . . .	Lord Byron *b.*—Pt.		
1789	*French Revolution*		The Regency Bill. French Revolution	
1791	. . . . . .	. . . . . .	. . . . . .	Custom House, Dublin
1792	*Convention*	Shelley *b.*—Pt.		
1793	. . . . . .	. . . . . .	Execution of Louis XVI. War with France	
1794	. . . . . .	. . . . . .	Victory off Ushant	
1795	*The Directory*	Keats *b.*—Pt. Carlyle *b.*—W.		
1796	. . . . . .	Corot *b.*—P.		
1797	. . . . . .	Schubert *b.*—M.	Battles of Cape St. Vincent and Camperdown	
1798	. . . . . .	Thomas Hood *b.*—Pt.	Battle of the Nile	
1799	*Napoleon Bonaparte First Consul*			

A.=Architect. P.=Painter. Pt.=Poet. S.=Sculptor. W.=Writer. M.=Musician.

121 Chart of the "Georgian" Period of Design, from 1700 to 1799

and the development of industry encouraged large masses of people to move from the country to the towns. At the same time, foreign imports were often interrupted by war. These conditions had a decisive effect on our system of farming and land-holding.

COSTUME

Let us begin our study of the eighteenth century by considering how people dressed. The early years of the period saw the advent of the coat and waistcoat. The long tunic and vest of Charles II's reign changed gradually into a waisted coat, wide in the skirts and stiffened with whalebone to make it stand out. The waistcoat, or vest, was still long and straight, and reached to the tops of the stockings, which were rolled over the breeches above the knee. The sleeves of the coat were still short, ending in wide cuffs, to show the full white shirt beneath.

The first male figure in our illustration (131) is probably a country gentleman; his dress therefore is sober; but a beau of the period was very ornate indeed; his coat of silk, satin, or velvet, elaborately laced. The beau's pocket contained a snuffbox with which he made great play; at his side he carried a slender sword and, under his arm, a clouded amber cane. Cravats were still much the same shape; and although, after the Battle of Steinkirk, a black stock came into fashion, called the "Steinkirk", the general form remained unchanged. Wigs were usually tied in the nape of the neck, and were called "tie wigs", those for dress occasions being perfumed, powdered, and curled; and over them three-cornered hats of dark felt were worn. While wigs were the mode, men's heads were close-shaven, and in the morning when they were at home, it was the custom to wear a nightcap, or sometimes a turban, instead of the wig, and a morning gown, or dressing-gown as we should now call it, often of beautiful material, and enriched with sumptuous embroidery.

122 A Soldier, 1742

The second figure in the illustration, a young girl, is evidently not a member of fashionable society. Her clothes are those of a well-to-do woman, possibly a squire's daughter, and though of fine material and colour, they include none of the exaggerated details seen at the Court and in the world of fashion. Her hair is dressed in ringlets, and is covered with a little lace cap and a wide straw hat. A high wig was often worn by ladies in town, with rows of curls above the forehead. Skirts also were more elaborate at the Court, and were much befrilled, and stretched out on hoops round the hips, with panniers of the material draped to the back, and falling in a tail to the hem of the dress. Queen Mary, wife of William III, set the fashion for wearing chintz and printed calicoes; and from that time an immense variety of variously patterned materials came into use. Hooded cloaks were still worn out of doors, and ladies went abroad in muddy weather in pattens and clogs. A very interesting collection of clogs and shoes can be seen in the Victoria and Albert Museum (124). Some of the pattens are covered in leather, and some with velvet sewn with gold braid; and often shoe and clog are made to match. As time went on, hoops became larger and head-dresses smaller; in 1744, when hoops reached their largest dimensions, the hair was closely dressed, and a little close-fitting cap was worn, often surmounted by a straw hat *à la bergère*. This corresponded with the "Watteau" period in France. But it did not last long; the craze for artificiality grew; and ladies' head-dresses grew in proportion. Greased,

123 A Soldier, 1742

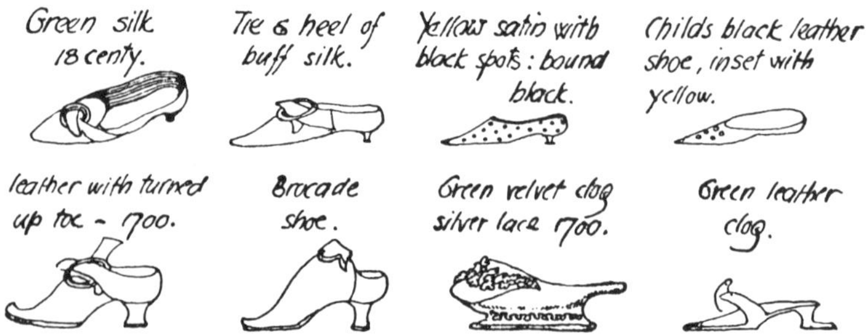

124 Shoes from the collection in the Victoria and Albert Museum, South Kensington

125 Bagnigge Wells, 1778

powdered, and curled, dressed high over enormous cushions, and surmounted by imitation fruit, flowers, and even ships, fashionable heads became so towering that women, when they travelled in sedan-chairs, were often obliged to keep the roof open. The fashionable lady, we are told, had no choice but to sleep in her head-dress. This she managed as best she could; and during the day a large mob-cap was worn over all, with ends that crossed beneath the chin, and tied at the back of the neck. Face-patches were worn by all. Hoops were smaller, as will be seen in the costume of the second lady, and ruching and pleating were much favoured. On looking at the gentleman with her, we see how coats have altered. Skirts gave place gradually to a tight coat, cut away into close-fitting tails. Knee-breeches were fastened over the stockings below the knee, and shoes had red heels. We have not space enough to describe all the different shapes of wigs and shoes that followed one another through the eighteenth century. For more detailed information, we must refer our readers to the splendid collection of costumes and accessories at the Victoria and Albert Museum.

In 1785 powder and mobs began to pall, and ladies affected curls and Leghorn hats, and the studied simplicity seen in Sir Joshua Reynolds's later portraits. Pantaloons, reaching to the middle of the calf, came in for men, and striped silks were worn on dress occasions. Men's own hair was worn long; and Charles James Fox, who led the fashion, dressed in a more careless and negligent fashion than had been seen before.

"I do not know the present generation by sight," Horace

Walpole wrote in 1791. Men "in their dirty shirts and shaggy hair have levelled nobility as much as the nobility in France have". A garment called the "Caroline wrapper" came into fashion, such as is seen on the last lady in our illustration—a garment still full in the skirts, but with the waist-line high, and tending slightly towards the classical form, which at the beginning of the nineteenth century became the rage.

In 1795 a tax on powder helped to kill the vogue of powdered hair; while swords ceased to be worn, and men began to carry umbrellas! Thus ended the age of powder, patches and brocade.

THE EIGHTEENTH-CENTURY NAVY

We have already noted how much Great Britain continued to depend on sea-power; and fig. 126 shows the *Royal George*, one of the famous ships of the period. Mounting 100 guns, her tonnage was 2,047; the length of keel 143 feet 5½ inches; beam, 51 feet 9½ inches; depth, 21 feet 6 inches. Built at Woolwich, she was launched in 1756, the year before William Pitt became War Minister, and sank at Spithead in 1782. The *Royal George* saw service under Admiral Hawke, and assisted in the defeat of the French at Belle-Isle in 1761.

Starting with the hull of the ship, we can still trace the old galley beak head, characteristic of sixteenth- and seventeenth-century vessels; but this feature was soon to disappear; and Nelson's flagship, the *Victory*, built 1775, has bows that form part of the hull in modern fashion—a loss from the picturesque point of view, but structurally an undoubted improvement. The forecastle is marked, and the poop, but neither of them is so pronounced as before. The three poop lanterns, with another in the main-top, gave by night the sign of a flag officer's ship. As to rigging, the *Royal George* has a spritsail under the bowsprit; but the sprit topmast and sail have gone, and the jackstaff takes its place for the flag. Triangular head-sails were also in use by this time; and by the middle of the eighteenth century stay-sails, on the stays between the masts, were common. The sailing diagram in our sixteenth-century chapter (14) explained how they were used, and how they held the ship in the wind for a longer period in coming round.

In the drawing we have square sails on the foremast and mainmast, and, on the mizzen, a lateen with square sails over. The

126 The *Royal George*

next development of the lateen was interesting. First, the fore part was cut off, turning it into a four-sided sail; then all the sail in front of the mast went, but the yard still projected. Then the yard in front was cut off; and by this time the sail had become the spanker, or driver. Then, about 1840, the Americans put a square sail in front of the driver, which was called the cross-jack. Head-sails made it necessary to add the jib-boom to the bowsprit; and the dolphin striker was placed underneath to embrace the whole and resist the strain of the head-sails.

Great art and cunning was required to handle an eighteenth-century warship, whether it was the *Royal George* or one of the vessels that Nelson commanded. At Trafalgar our sailors had to depend on guns with a range of only 400 to 600 yards, and they merely lobbed shot at the French. We lost 1,609 killed, wounded, and drowned, the French 4,528, the Spaniards 2,405, and no ships were sunk. Nowadays, the torpedo has a range of four to five sea miles. At the Battle of Jutland, on May 31st, 1916, which like Trafalgar was a turning-point in a great war, Beatty opened fire at about 18,500 yards, and the gunners fired at a smudge on the horizon they imagined to be the enemy.

In the catalogue of the Naval and Marine Engineering Collection in the Science Museum at South Kensington, there is an illuminating note on eighteenth-century ship-design.

> A great obstacle to progress [we read] was created in 1719 by the English Navy Board, who, satisfied with the performances of existing types of vessels, laid down a fixed scale of dimensions and tonnage for ships of each class, thus leaving no power with the designers of adapting the vessel's displacement to the increasing weight of armament and other changes. This remained in force for nearly a century, until the demonstrated superiority of French vessels of equal rating initiated a greatly improved scale of dimensions.

Standardisation, in fact, spelt stagnation during the eighteenth century, as it does today.

The next illustration(127) is of a tea clipper, dating from about the middle of the nineteenth century, so that properly speaking it is outside our period; but, as the clipper marked the final development of the sailing ship before steam came in, we

127 A Tea Clipper

felt that it must be illustrated. Earlier trading ships had been of a shorter and more tubby build, not more than four times the beam in length; the clipper was five to six; and the lines of the hull were as beautiful as those of a modern yacht. The gracefully rising bows show that the boat could sail into the wind. The clipper carried a tremendous spread of canvas. Starting with the head-sails, we have three of these, though sometimes four were carried, the lower being the fore-topmost stay-sail, then inner, outer, and flying jib. The jib-boom, braced with the dolphin striker underneath, is shown in the sketch. The foremast and mainmast have their foresail and mainsail; and these with the mizzen are well fitted with topsails, top-gallants, and royals. At the stern there is the driver, or spanker, the lineal descendant of the fifteenth-century lateen. Stay-sails were fitted on the stays between the masts, and studding-sails on booms projected from the yards of the square sails. Here the art of sailing reaches its highest point. The clipper was good before the wind thanks to her square sails, and could steal into the wind with the aid of her head- and stay-sails and spanker. We shall be referring to the tea clippers again in our volume on the nineteenth century.

INDUSTRY AND INVENTION

We have seen how, during earlier periods, man was always in search of new mechanical devices, to replace or simplify the work of his hands; but until the eighteenth century wind and water were the only sources of power he had learned to use. The introduction of steam as a practical form of power revolutionised world history.

Among the developments we have to describe is that of the power-loom; but first let us glance at the primitive hand spinning-wheel. This beautiful little machine (128) was introduced in the sixteenth century, and took the place of spinning by a handle spindle as described in Vol. I, Chapter IV. The right foot, acting on a treadle, turned the wheel by the connecting-rod and cranked arm to the wheel axle. The wheel, by driving bands, turned a horizontal spindle; and it required a certain degree of practice to keep the wheel turning regularly, and prevent it from reversing. The spindle was fitted with a pair of wooden wings called fliers, and fitted with little wire hooks; there was a reel on the spindle, and a small grooved wooden wheel which took up the drive from the driving-wheel. As to the method of spinning, the preparation of the carded wool was described in Vol. I. A short length of yarn, already spun from the wool, was threaded through the hollow end of the spindle, and passed out of a hole in the side; it was then threaded through the wire hooks in the fliers, and tied to the reel. The thread was wound on to the reel as it was turned by the wheel, and the twist that is necessary to make the yarn was given by the action of the fliers. If a piece of darning-wool is pulled to pieces, it will be found to consist of many short hairs of varying lengths, bound together by twisting. So, in spinning, some carded wool was put on a distaff placed on the wheel framing, or a portion called a rolag was held in the hand; and the art of spinning consisted in feeding out the wool, so that a thread of even thickness was twisted by the action of the fliers. String, rope, and all sorts of threads are made in this way. Now that we have learned how yarn used to be spun, we can go on to consider the various changes that took place during the eighteenth century.

128 Spinning

In the first half of the century, the masters found the yarn, and gave the work out to the hand-loom weavers, who did their work at home, or in their own little workshops, and, though they were obliged to work hard, had the satisfaction of feeling that they were their own masters. The yarn was made by spinners;

and it took ten spinners to keep one weaver at work. Attempts were made to remedy this state of affairs; and in 1764 Hargreaves invented the spinning-jenny, which consisted of a horizontal fly-wheel, driving as many as eight vertical spindles and fliers. The machine was worked by hand, and enabled the spinner to keep pace with the weaver. Arkwright still further improved spinning; and in 1779 Crompton perfected what was called a "mule", which, by incorporating the good points of Hargreaves' jenny and Arkwright's machine, enabled the spinner to produce yarn faster than the weaver could weave it. Side by side with the spinners, the weavers were improving their looms; and it was Kay's invention of the fly-shuttle that was the first step in the chain of invention, because it at once doubled the weavers' output. Before this date, the loom was worked as described in Vol. I, Chapter IV, and the shuttle, with its weft, had been thrown by hand from side to side through the warp; in the fly-shuttle this operation was reproduced by a mechanical arrangement.

129 Bristol Ware

With the addition of the fly-shuttle, the loom remained as before, until, in 1785, a clergyman, Cartwright by name, who, until he visited Arkwright's mill had never seen a loom, invented one worked by water-power. Then in 1789 Cartwright, who had now set up a factory himself, installed a steam-engine.

Primitive steam-engines had been used since the end of the seventeenth century—notably Thomas Savery's of about 1700, a kind of steam vacuum pump with elliptical

130 A Lead Rain-water Head, from Compton Wynyates, Warwickshire

receivers, which looked rather like a hydraulic ram, and was used for pumping water from mines. But it was James Watt who about 1776 finally perfected this form of power. In 1777 he wrote to his partner of a pumping-engine he had set up in Cornwall: "The velocity, violence magnitude, and horrible noise of the engine give universal satisfaction to all beholders." During the close of the eighteenth century the new form of power was rapidly applied to flour-, saw-, and silk-mills, and the reign of wind- and water-power was over.

We have seen how the wars of the eighteenth century enlarged our empire and developed trade. As our colonists went out to the new countries, they sent home raw materials, and took in exchange the goods manufactured from them. It was a time of great expansion, and speculation was rife. Many businessmen saw the chance of making fortunes; and the pity was that in doing so they inflicted great hardship on others. The introduction of new machinery, for example, ruined many of the handicraftsmen, who were perhaps too old, or too conservative, to take to the new methods. Formerly the weavers had done their work at home, and this was possible when they themselves supplied the power that worked the hand-looms, but it became impossible when the steam-engine worked the power-loom. Every workman then had to come to the factory where the source of power lay, and the new industrial centres were established without any

131 Costume of the Eighteenth Century

regard for what are called "the amenities of existence". Cottages had to be built close to the mills, and, as people were so anxious to get rich, they had not time to think about light and air, sunlight and health, so the squalid industrial town sprang up, with all its problems affecting life and happiness. It was not until 1909 that the government of that day brought in a Town Planning Act, which specified that "amenity", or the quality of being pleasant and agreeable, must be considered in planning towns and building houses.

FARMING

Not only were the many wars of the eighteenth century a draw on Great Britain's manpower; but they checked the flow of foreign imports. Meanwhile industrial developments drew men from the country to the new factories and towns, so that the farmer faced a double problem—how to produce a larger supply of foodstuffs with the help of fewer men.

We have already referred to the process of land-enclosure that had been going on since the end of the Middle Ages. The eighteenth century was to see its culmination; but the old open-field system of agriculture (see p. 58) still existed over very large areas. Improved methods of farming, however, were being advocated by agricultural experts; and in his book *Horse-Hoeing Husbandry*, published in 1733, Jethro Tull recommended careful selection of seed, and planting in furrows instead of broadcast, so that the land could be hoed and cultivated in between the rows. The old farmers on the open-field system were too conservative to adopt his methods; and it was left to the larger landowners, working as individuals, to demonstrate the soundness of Tull's teaching. Lord Townshend was another pioneer. We have already enjoyed our glimpse of his family house, Raynham Hall, Norfolk(75, 77), built by his ancestor, Sir Roger Townshend, in 1636. It was for this Lord Townshend that Kent remodelled the house (p. 124). Townshend believed in alternating turnips, grasses, and corn; and by so doing he provided winter food for his cattle, and avoided having to let the land lie fallow once in three years, as the open-field farmer did. He is also reputed to have introduced "marling" and so transformed the fertility of some of the difficult light Norfolk soils. More stock could be kept, which meant more manure to fertilise the soil, and so increased production of both corn and meat. Townshend's methods were so successful that he was mockingly nicknamed "Turnip", though it was soundly suggested that the term would be more fittingly applied to the heads of those who sneered at him.

Arthur Young (1741–1820), a great advocate of enclosures, gives the following description of a specimen of Townshend's handiwork:

> Thirty years ago it was an extensive heath without tree or shrub, only a sheep walk to another farm. Such a number of carriages crossed it, that they would sometimes be a mile apart in pursuit of the best track. Now there is an excellent turnpike road, enclosed on each side with a good quick-set hedge, and the whole laid out in enclosures and

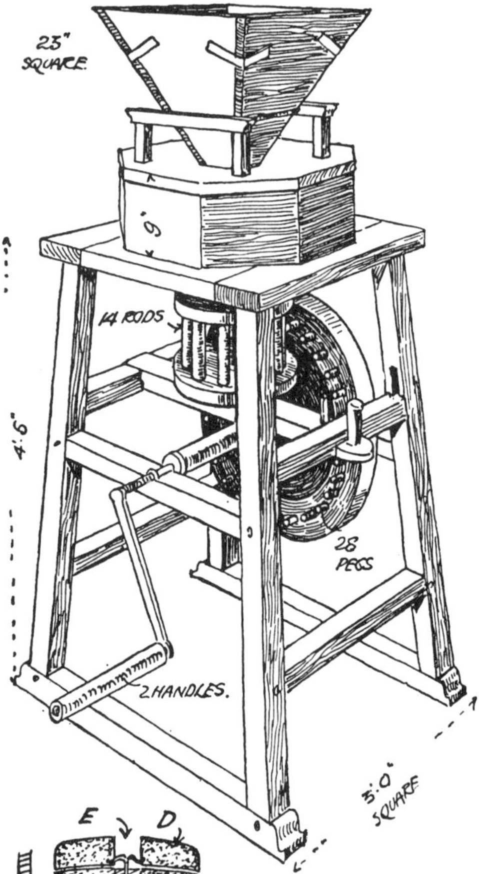

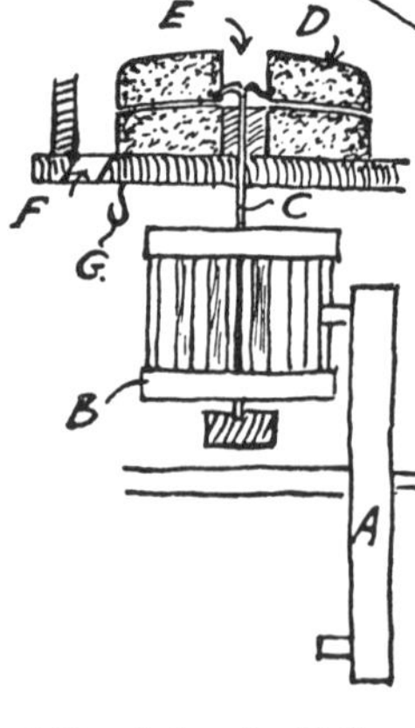

Flywheel *A* turns cogged wheel *B*. Spindle *C* is attached to this and Top Stone *D*. Corn fed in at *E* is passed between the stones and the flour comes out through *F* into sack hung on hook *G*

132 A handmill from Long Crichel, Dorset, now in the Pitt Rivers Museum, Farnham

cultivated on the Norfolk system in superior style. The whole is let at 15*s*. an acre, ten times the original value.

Young became the Secretary of the Board of Agriculture in 1793. He advocated reclaiming the wastes, breaking up commons, and doing away with the open-field system; and between 1793 and 1809 it is believed that about 4½ million acres were added to cultivation in this way. The Napoleonic Wars made such a policy imperative; and the open-field system was doomed when it was discovered that by enclosure the country could be fed; but great hardship was inflicted on the small copy-holders, who held a few acres in the common fields, with grazing rights on the commons and wastes. They led a healthy, interesting life, and were sturdy types. Too often their small holding was taken from them, as More had said earlier, by "coveyne and fraude", and they drifted into the towns to swell the volume of misery there, and to create new problems for later generations.

Bakewell, a Leicestershire farmer, born in 1725, greatly improved sheep- and cattle-breeding, increased the size of the stock and consequently their production of meat.

Fig. 133 gives some of the eighteenth-century types of plough. Small, who made No. 2, established works in Berwickshire in 1763, and died about 1793. He was the first to invent a cast-iron turn furrow. No. 3 is interesting, because it was probably the first iron plough. Young, in his Agricultural Report on Suffolk in 1804, mentions a plough made of iron by a "very ingenious blacksmith of the name of Brand . . . no other in the kingdom equal to it". Brand died at the end of the eighteenth century. Nos. 1, 2, and 3 are all swing ploughs. The plough head was an important part of this implement; the depth of the furrow was regulated by the position at which the pull was applied here, or by the ploughman lifting, or bearing, on the handles. The Rutland plough was of this swing type, with the addition of a land and furrow wheel at the end of its beam. The swing plough was more suitable for the use of the tenant-farmers, to whom the land was let after the enclosures. In the old open-field system a far heavier plough could be used, and pulled by all the village oxen yoked together.

There is much more in the technique of ploughing than at first meets the eye. The ploughman begins by measuring out the field in strips a chain wide, by putting in sticks against each

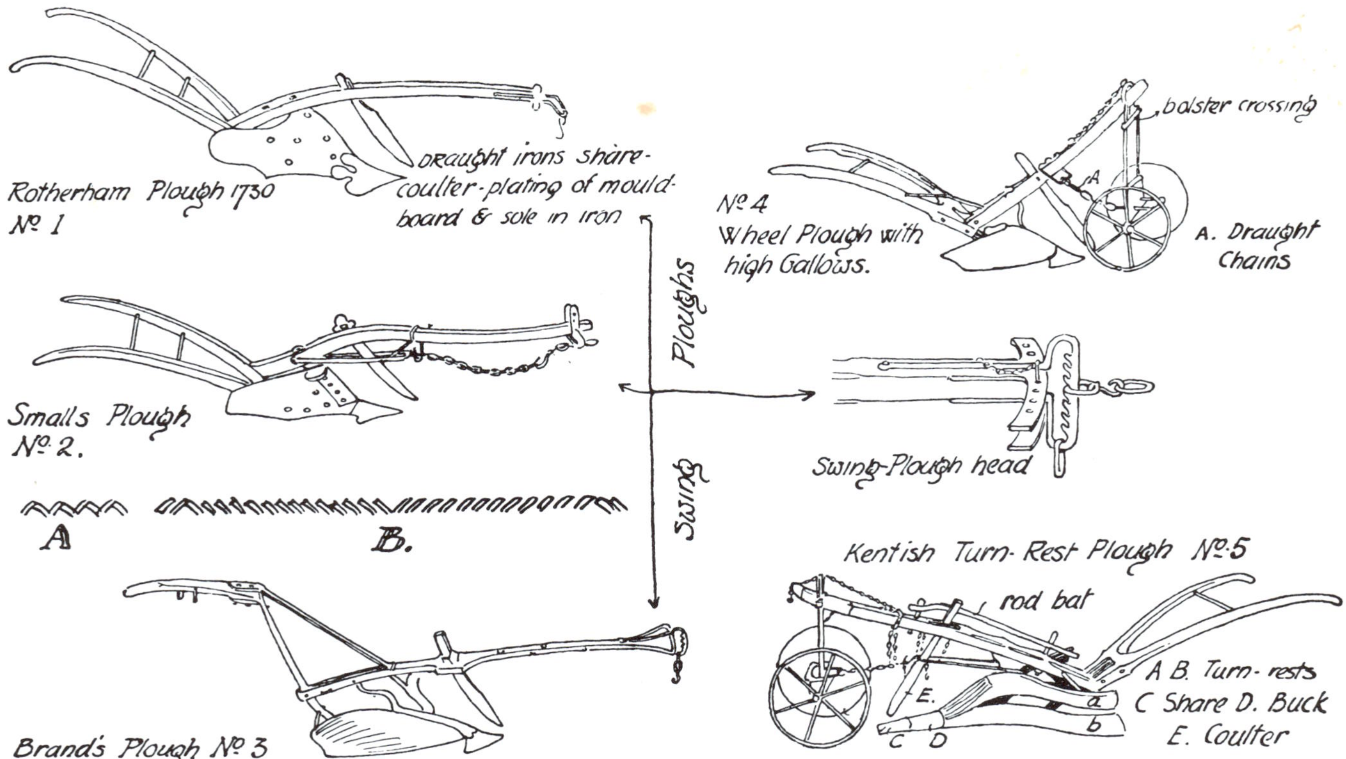

133 Eighteenth-century Types of Ploughs

hedgerow. Remember, by the way, that a chain is the length of a cricket pitch, or four rods, which is the countryman's great measure. The ploughman starts by ploughing from one stick to another; and, if he is a good man, he keeps an absolutely straight line. He does not plough the next furrow immediately alongside the first, because this would resolve itself into a series of ridges as fig. 133, *A*; instead, he proceeds along the hedgerow, his path being called the headland, and strikes the next furrow up from the stick a chain away from the first. In this way he produces the effect shown in *B*. The point where the slices cut by the plough incline and meet together is the ridge, and where they part the furrow. These furrows are used for drainage; on wet ground they might be closer together than a chain. Where ploughed land has been put down to grass, you can still trace the line of the old water furrows; and in the late afternoon, with a low sun, the field has a corrugated look.

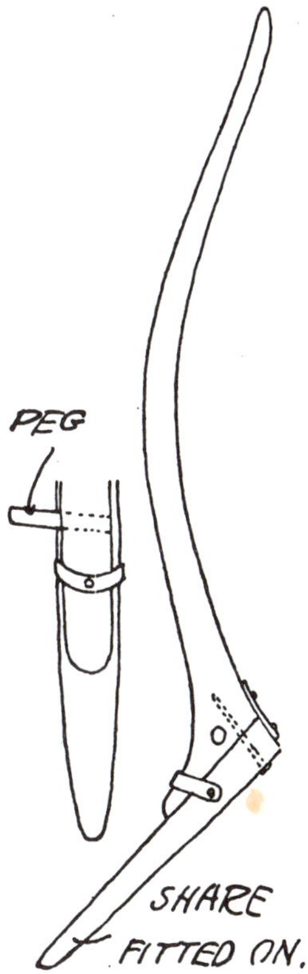

134 Hand-Plough, West Highlands

Fig. 133, No. 4, is an interesting type used in East Anglia. The set of the plough was adjusted by the draught chains. The Kentish turn-rest plough, No. 5, was an exception to this rule, and was designed to lay all the furrow slices in one direction. This was very useful on the side of sloping downs, and the plough went up and down and cut the furrow slices side by side, without any journeys across the headlands. It was arranged in this way. The turn-rest *B* was removable and reversible; so, at the end of the furrow, it was taken off, and put on the other side of the plough; and the coulter was adjustable and kept in position by the rod bat. With this form of ploughing you did not get ridge and water furrows.

The last plough we propose to mention is the hand-plough

(134), which was, and still is, used in the West Highlands. Fig. 137, which shows how the implement was used, was made from a sketch in *Harper's Magazine*, 1885–6, where it is described as the "Crooked Spade" used in Cape Breton by descendants of settlers from the north of Scotland.

To round off the subject of ploughing, here is a poetic toast, in which the speaker is an eighteenth-century farmer:

Let the wealthy and great
Roll in splendour and state,
I envy them not, I declare it;
I eat my own lamb,
My chickens and ham,
I shear my own fleece and I wear it.
I have lawns, I have bowers,
I have fruit, I have flowers,
The lark is my morning alarmer;
So my jolly boys now,
Here's God speed the plough,
Long life and success to the farmer.

Verses like these, with farming scenes, are often lettered on eighteenth-century china mugs.

After the corn was grown and reaped, it was carried to the barn and threshed with flails, as shown in fig. 25. Jethro Tull (1730) is credited with having been the first to invent a threshing-machine; he was "wicked enough to construct a machine which, by working a set of sticks, beat out the corn without manual labour". Fig. 136 gives the detail of the handstaff and swingel of the flail. Made by an old labourer with wood cut out of the hedgerow, his jack-knife, and an old boot, it is a clever anticipation of a universal joint.

135 The "Crooked Spade"

Now we reach the last of our series of windmills (137). This

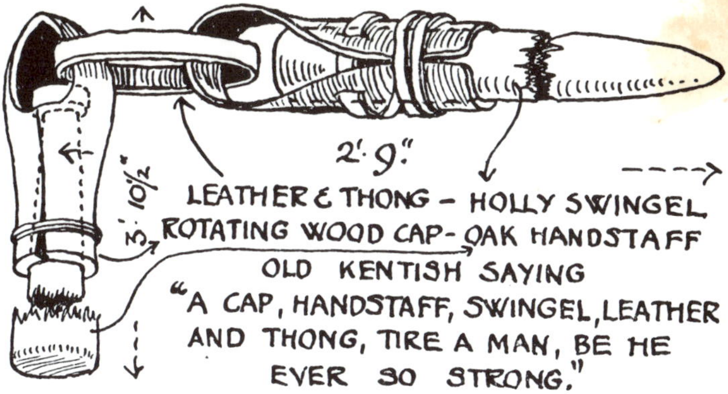

136 Details of the Flail

type was called the tower mill, its mechanism being the same as that described on p. 170. This sketch shows how the louvres to the sails are not all fixed in one and the same plane. The louvres are shown open; but, when closed, they would form a nearly continuous surface, with a twist in each sail rather like that in the blades of a maritime propeller. If you examine the drawing, you will see how the wind, acting on these sails, would rotate them in an anti-clockwise direction. The brick tower is an extraordinarily fine piece of work. The lower plan is octagonal, with the external angles taken off, and the upper stage is developed, in a very simple way, into a regular sixteen-sided figure. The old bricklayer who built it must have been a fine craftsman.

THE EIGHTEENTH-CENTURY HOUSE

It is obvious that the methods so successfully adopted by experts like Townshend and Bakewell, although they may have harmed the small owners, were remarkably advantageous to the large landlords. Great fortunes were made. The fact that land could be let at ten times the original value meant greatly increased rent rolls; so we find that many very wonderful country houses were built at this time. Judged by plan alone, it is true, they are not especially interesting. The layout usually consisted of a central portion containing the reception rooms, with the stables in one wing, connected by a colonnade with the main building, and the kitchens in another. Such a house is

137 A Tower Mill

described on p. 209 (also fig. 79) and there is no evidence of any regard for the comfort of the householder's servants. Their part of the house was the basement; and in one of Robert Adam's villas the kitchens are built in a pit, sunk in the ground at some little distance, and connected with the basement of the house by a subterranean tunnel. The eighteenth-century great house was not nearly so human or practical as that of Elizabeth's time, where difficulties were not dodged but grappled with. The key-note of eighteenth-century architecture was often display.

We emphasise these points because some of our readers may intend to become architects; and them we would remind that architecture is a practical art. If they can arrange a house in which a family can live in comfort, into the rooms of which the sun will shine, from which dirt and disease are kept away, they will have rendered good service. If they can do this, and add beauty, they will also be great architects.

The eighteenth century, however, excelled in the production of more modest houses—the pleasant old-fashioned places that still add distinction to the streets of almost any English country town. The doctor generally lives in one, and the lawyer will have another. The walls are faced with red bricks that have weathered to a delightful mellowness; the sash-windows are of pleasant proportions, disposed in a regular way. There is a good robust cornice, which provides a brim to the roof; and in the roof are dormer-windows. The doorways are always interesting; and there may be some fine iron railings and gates. Indoors, the basement kitchen is generally avoided, and the rooms are planned for comfort rather than for display. Walls are pleasantly panelled, and the staircases good. They are eminently houses to live in.

Fig. 138 shows a house built right at the beginning of the eighteenth century in 1701. It may have been designed by Wren or one of his pupils; and undoubtedly it was taken as a model for the other houses of this type to which we have referred, though this particular one is built of stone. It is known as Mompesson House, and was for long the Judge's Lodging. Inside are some good interiors and a very fine staircase. In design this house is very simple and unpretentious, yet full of dignity. It is beautifully proportioned, and the spacing of the windows is admirable. The plain walling surfaces at the sides are

138 An Early Eighteenth-century House, in The Close, Salisbury

used in contrast to the richer treatment of door and window over; and the composition is bound together by the cornice. Across the whole front is spun a web of beautiful wrought ironwork, which shows against the stone like so much lace; and these railings, against its sober frontage, give just the right effect of richness and plainness combined. The roof is covered with red tiles; and it should be noticed that the shape of the house is an oblong, which can be covered with plain slopes, hipped at the angles, without any gables. We saw in the Middle Ages how the house started as a hall with a roof of its own, around which were grouped the solar at one end and the kitchen at the other, and the appearance was rather that of a collection of buildings grouped together. Our present illustration shows how in the course of centuries these all merged into one building, under one roof.

The windows of the house also deserve study. Up till now we have only seen the casement variety, where the opening part, generally in iron, was hinged at the side like a door. In fig. 138 we meet for the first time what are known as sash-windows.

Those at Raynham Hall(75) were inserted about 1730, nearly a century after the house was built. The frames are hollow boxes used to conceal weights, which, with lines running over pulleys, counterbalance the sash. This type of window was not used in England until the end of the seventeenth century; but from a book called *A Journey to Paris*, published in 1698, we learn that they were regarded as an English invention:

> The Marchal very obligingly showed us his own apartment, for all the rest of the house was full of workmen. He showed us his great sash windows; how easily they might be lifted up and down, and stood at any height, which contrivance he said he had out of England, by a small model brought on purpose from thence, there being nothing of this poise in windows in France before.

The problem of providing windows has had a great deal to do with the architectural appearance of houses. From Gothic times down to the Jacobean Age, windows were formed by placing openings side by side, the stone or wood division between being called a mullion; sometimes they were divided in their height by horizontal transoms. It was a very useful type, because one could arrange windows to almost any size, by bringing the requisite number of openings or units together. The glazing was in small pieces of glass, leaded up either in plain oblongs, diamond-shaped lozenges, or pretty geometrical patterns. Inigo Jones does not seem to have troubled very much about the filling-in and glazing of his windows, and used wooden frames and casement-windows with lead glazing. Then came sash-windows, in which the sashes were divided up by wooden bars, which necessitated the use of larger sheets of glass than were required for lead glazing. The French, though we gather that they experimented with these, never adopted them, and still use large casement-windows, generally opening inwards with a fanlight over. The old glass was blown, and has pleasant peculiarities. A blow-pipe was put into a crucible of molten glass(104), and a sufficient quantity brought on to the end. This was blown, and then the blow-pipe was rapidly twisted round and round, with the result that a large thin disc was formed at the end. From the outer parts were cut the panes of glass for the windows; but the centre, where it had been attached to the blow-pipe, was thicker, and had a knot when broken off, which formed the bull's-eye one sometimes sees in old windows. This old blown glass is not quite regular, but looks attractive in use, and gives the house a lively appearance. As one walks past, the light is caught and reflected from the different surfaces, not all in the same plane.

Fig. 139 shows a town house of about 1771, typical of the work of Robert Adam. The exteriors of his houses were generally very simple, depending for effect on a skilful disposition of well-proportioned windows; there might be a string-course at the level of the window-sills, and the front of the house was usually finished with a good cornice. The small amount of ornament used was centred on the doorway. In this case we have fluted columns of the Doric order, and in the entablature over, the lower member called the architrave has been omitted, with the result that the frieze rests directly on the top member, or abacus, of the cap to the column. This kind of ornament, and the graceful

139 A Town House of the Later Eighteenth Century
Chandos House, Queen Anne Street, London. By Robert Adam, 1771

fanlight over the door, are typical of Adam's work. The front railings should be noticed, with the lantern-holders, which were necessary before the days of gas; on the standards supporting them are cone-shaped link-extinguishers. The link-boy, when he had lighted you home, extinguished his link by pushing it up into the cone. The chairmen, with their sedan, show a common method of going about London in the eighteenth century. There is still a public house in Mayfair called "The Two Chairmen" which used to be frequented by upper-class servants; and there is another called "The Running Footman".

The eighteenth century was a great time for the amateur architect. No rich young man's education was thought to be complete unless he had made the Grand Tour. And cultured travellers came back from Italy full of contempt for their old homes, and proceeded to dot about on the countryside exact reproductions of Italian villas. Practical considerations were abandoned, and no house was thought fit to live in unless it followed the rules laid down by Palladio, an Italian architect, born in Vicenza in 1518, where he did most of his work, and who died in 1580. Architecture became an exact art, and a matter of rule; and the amateur designed houses according to Palladio, on the rules laid down in Gibbs's *Book of Architecture*, 1728, or Isaac Ware's *Compleat Body of Architecture*, 1756.

Among the most brilliant of these amateurs was the celebrated Lord Burlington, who gathered around him a circle of gifted men at Burlington House, Piccadilly, and Chiswick House, his Thames-side villa—both of them buildings that he had helped to design and decorate himself.

There is an interesting account of Buckingham House, built in 1705, which stood on the present site of Buckingham Palace, looking down the Mall. Bought by George III in 1762, and afterwards known as the Queen's Palace, it had a central block, and side wings, connected with open colonnades. This is how the ducal owner described his home and daily life.

> I rise now in summer about seven o'clock, from a very large bedchamber, entirely quiet, high, and free from the early sun, to walk in the gardens . . . my iron palisade that encompasses a square court, which has in the midst a great basin with statues and waterworks, and, from its entrance, rises all the way imperceptibly, till we mount to a terrace in front of the hall.

At the sides of the court were two wings joined to the house

> by corridores, supported by Ionic pillars. In one of these wings is a large kitchen thirty feet high, with an open cupola on the top: near it are a larder, brewhouse, and laundry, with rooms over them for servants; the upper sort of servants are lodged in the older wing, which has also here wardrobes and a storeroom for fruit. On the top of all, a leaden cistern, holding fifty tons of water, driven up by an engine from the Thames, supplies all the waterworks in the courts and gardens, which lie quite round the house, and through one of which a grass walk conducts to the stables, built round a court, with six coach-houses and forty stalls.
>
> To the gardens we go down from the house by seven steps, into a gravel walk that reaches across the garden, with a covered arbour at each end of it. Another, of thirty feet broad, leads from the front of the house, and lies between two groves of tall lime trees, planted in several equal ranks, upon a carpet of grass: the outsides of these groves are bordered with tubs of bays and orange trees. At the end of this broad walk, you go up to a terrace four hundred paces long, with a large semicircle in the middle, from whence are beheld the queen's two parks, and a great part of Surrey: then going down a few steps, you walk on the banks of a canal six hundred yards long and seventeen broad, with two rows of limes on each side of it.
>
> On one side of this terrace a wall, covered with roses and jessamines, is made low, to admit the view of a meadow, full of cattle; and at each end a descent into parterres, with fountains and waterworks. From the biggest of these parterres we pass into a little square garden, that has a fountain in the middle, and two greenhouses on the sides, with a convenient bathing apartment in one of them, and near another part of it lies a flower garden. Below all this, a kitchen garden, full of the best sorts of fruits, has several walks in it fit for the coldest weather.

So far as the inside of the house was concerned, the entrance court led into

> a large hall . . . the walls of it covered with a set of pictures done in the school of Raphael. Out of this, on the right hand, we go into a parlour, thirty-three feet by thirty-nine. . . . From hence we pass, through a suite of large rooms, into a bedchamber of thirty-four feet by twenty-seven; within it a large closet, that opens into a greenhouse. On the left hand of the hall . . . we go up eight-and-forty steps, ten feet broad. . . . The roof of this staircase, which is fifty-five feet from the ground, is forty feet by thirty-six, and filled

140 The Great Room at Kenwood, Highgate, North London, Designed by Robert Adam in 1767

> with the figures of gods and goddesses. . . . From a wide landing-place on the stair's-head, a great double door opens into an apartment of the same dimensions with that below, only three feet higher. . . .

The saloon on this floor was 35 feet high, 36 feet broad, and 45 feet long; and you could have put the whole of a moderate-sized modern house into that one room.

Fig. 140 is of the great room at Kenwood, designed by Robert Adam in 1767 for Lord Mansfield, and now open to the public. The columns shown in the foreground have Corinthian caps; and a very beautiful effect has been obtained by placing these in the open, and taking the entablature over it across the front of the apsidal semicircular recesses at the ends of the hall. The apses are finished with half-domed ceilings, which pick up the same line as the circular vault over the main body of the hall. This vault is beautifully decorated, and the panels are filled with paintings. Altogether, a very appropriate background for the fine ladies and gentlemen shown in the picture. Before leaving Kenwood, we should like to point out that the architectural detail is daintier and more graceful than the work of the first half of the century, and that the ornament, with its use of the "honeysuckle" design, gives an early indication of the Greek Revival, which followed the publication, in 1762, of Stuart and Revett's book on the *Antiquities of Athens*. Meanwhile the Middle Ages were coming back into fashion; and Horace Walpole had begun building himself a house, Strawberry Hill, Twickenham, in the Gothic manner. Eventually Greek and Gothic were destined to triumph over Palladian.

The next illustration (141) is of a staircase; and it has been selected because it shows, like the first one illustrated in Vol. I, Chapter I, a circular treatment, though the centre stone newel in this case is missing, and the balustrade is of iron. Sir Christopher Wren constructed a very beautiful circular staircase at St. Paul's Cathedral. The steps were solid blocks of stone, with a moulded nosing worked on the front edge, and returned at the ends; and the steps, cut radiating to the centre, were built into the wall at one end, so that each step becomes a cantilever, the front edge of one resting on the back edge of the next below—an extremely elegant and structurally sound method of construction. All sorts of designs were used in connection with the

141 Staircase, late Eighteenth Century
Founded on Barrow Hall, Essex

iron balustrade. The King's Staircase at Hampton Court is the work of the great smith Jean Tijou (p. 162), who was employed by Wren; and here the treatment consists of panels filled in with scrolls and foliage, which repeat up the staircase; but the junction between the panels is not very noticeable, and the effect that of a continuous pattern of splendid wrought ironwork. Later, the balustrade became a succession of single balusters; and the favourite patterns for balusters were based on a lyre, or S-shaped. The former have been shown on the drawing, and are alternated with plain bars, the handrail being in mahogany. We should explain, by the way, that the little boy under the stairs is not weeping, but hiding from his sister, and has been drawn in this position, because we know of another today who used to imagine that it somehow rendered him invisible.

FURNITURE

We have written of the great houses and of the beautiful interior decoration of the eighteenth century; and we must now look at the furniture that filled the rooms. Towards the end of

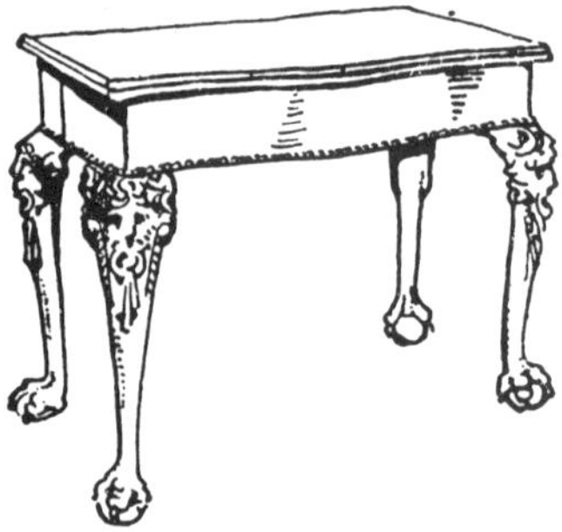

142 A Carved Side-table, 1735

the seventeenth century, oak gave way to other woods. Painted beech was used, and walnut. The Portuguese leather-back chair of the reign of Charles II, made in compliment to his wife, Catherine of Braganza, was replaced by furniture showing the strong Dutch influence that reached England during the reign of William and Mary. In the time of homely Queen Anne, walnut was the favourite wood, and furniture began to lose its ponderous proportions and to take on a line more conducive to comfort. Mahogany was regarded as a luxury, although at least one set of mahogany chairs is still in existence, thought to have been made as early as 1715.

In eighteenth-century furniture, for the first time, we see the mark of the individual artist. It is no longer classified according to its period alone, but according to the man who made it; for great designers had arisen, each the creator of a separate style. Three names spring into prominence—Chippendale, Hepplewhite, and Sheraton. Chippendale and his school held sway from 1750 until 1780. The mahogany chair of 1750(143) is a good example of his work, its decoration being founded on the acanthus leaf. The table(142), made a little earlier, about 1735, is in walnut, has masks carved on the knees of the legs, and ball and claw feet. It is generally supposed that the ball and claw feet are an adaptation from the Oriental design of a dragon's claw clasping a pearl. Chippendale's genius was such that he took many apparently incongruous motifs and welded them into one harmonious design.

While speaking of furniture, we must not forget the hangings and the embroidery—an art at which the modern woman may well marvel. There existed also the great tapestry factory at Mortlake, which produced cushions and bed-hangings and daybeds of tapestry similar to those of Gobelins.

Many books of furniture were brought out, with engraved plates illustrating the designs of furniture-makers, famous or less well known to the general public.

143 A Chippendale Chair, 1750

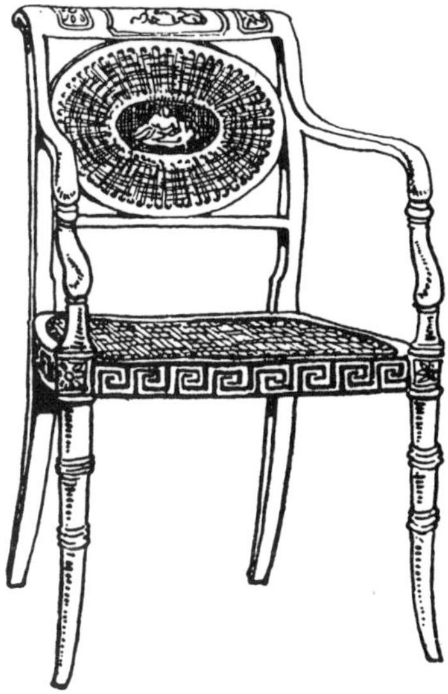

144 A Cane-back Chair with Painted Panels, 1800

Kent, of course, was widely celebrated, but the designers whose work appeared also included Manwaring, Ince, Mayhew, Johnson, and others.

Hepplewhite, who practised from 1775 to 1795, evolved a more delicate type of furniture. He used inlay, both in pattern and line in various woods; and his furniture is less solid and more elegant than that of his predecessor and rival. He was influenced by the Adam brothers, and affected a more classical line than Chippendale. Fig. 148 is of mahogany inlaid with boxwood, made in 1775; the shield-shaped back is very typical of this school. The table (145),

145 A Hepplewhite carved Pier-Table, 1775

of 1775, is a pier-table of mahogany, very delicately carved in low relief; but this is an exceptional piece, in that it is carved and not inlaid. Generally the pattern and colour was achieved by inlay; and many woods were used, such as tulipwood, walnut, sycamore, boxwood, satinwood, rosewood, and pear.

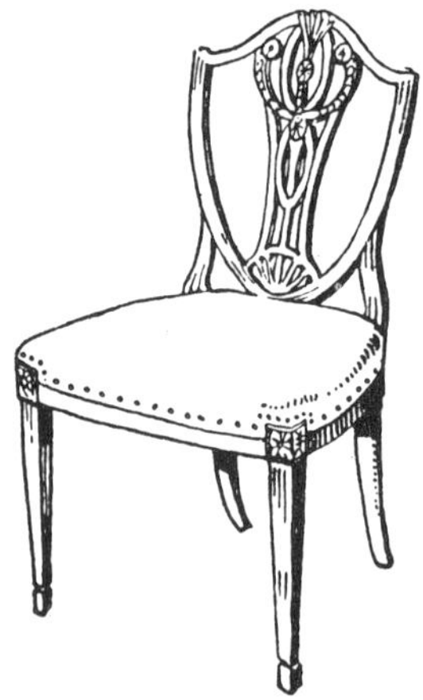

146 A Hepplewhite Shield-back Chair, 1775

Sheraton, whose influence was active from 1790 until 1805, though certainly great in his earlier, more restrained and classical work, marks the decline and fall of the art of furniture design His last efforts, strange and often bizarre, tell of the decay of a great mind; and from 1805 onwards we must gradually resign ourselves to the horrors of the mahogany Victorian era.

The little table(147) was made in the year 1790. It is of mahogany, one of the new little "tea-tables" then so fashionable in the polite world. It has a fragile grace that is all its own; and so has the chair(144) of 1800. It is of painted beech, with cane back and seat, and miniature painted scenes by way of ornament. Thanks to the classical taste of the period, it still retains a feeling of symmetry.

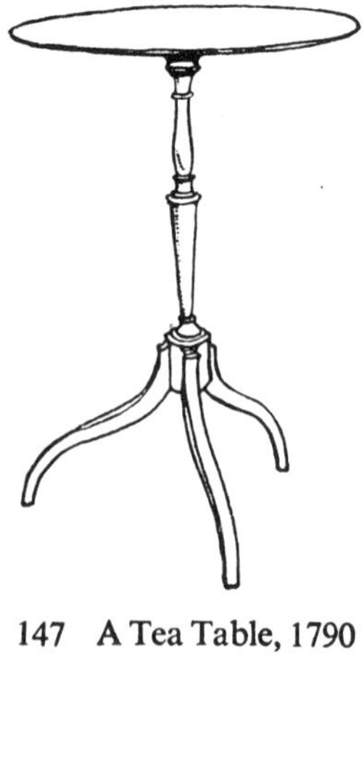

147 A Tea Table, 1790

Fig. 148 is of a tent-bed, so called for the obvious reason that its shape suggested a tent. Such beds were, of course, considerably cheaper than those made of mahogany, with elaborately turned, fluted, and carved posts and tester. The latter followed the lines of the sixteenth-century bed(37), but were lighter and more graceful in detail. With the tent-bed it was only necessary to have a light iron framework to support the hangings, and little brass finials showing above. There is a bed of this type at the

148 A Tent-Bed

Victoria and Albert Museum, South Kensington, that once belonged to David Garrick; but tent-beds were generally found in less important houses. They were used well on into the nineteenth century, and perhaps their framework suggested the terrible brass-bound iron bedsteads of Victorian times. A tent-bed is shown in one of the illustrations to *Dame Wiggins of Lee and Her Seven Wonderful Cats*, a nursery-rhyme saga, with many interesting glimpses of cottage-life, published in **1823.** Here is one of the verses:

While she ran to the field
  To look for its dam,
They were warming the bed
  For the poor sick lamb:
They turn'd up the clothes
  All as neat as could be;
"I shall ne'er want a nurse,"
  Said Dame Wiggins of Lee.

Five of her cats are shown airing the sheets with a warming-pan; one is assisting the "poor sick lamb" into the tent-bed, and the other is holding the nightcap that everybody wore.

MUSICAL INSTRUMENTS

We conclude our long series of musical instruments, from the sixteenth-century harp(40), with an illustration of an early piano(149) made at the end of the eighteenth century.

149 A Piano, End of the Eighteenth Century

150 First part of "Under the Greenwood Tree"

151 Second part of "Under the Greenwood Tree"

Pianos were invented in 1709 by a Florentine; and the distinctive difference between them and harpsichords and virginals is that the strings are struck by little hammers in the former, and in the latter plucked. The harpsichord, as its name would suggest, was nearer of kin to the harp than the piano; but they are all related.

The keyboard of the early piano consisted of balanced levers, which, struck at one end by the finger, raised at the other a contrivance called the damper. This damper could also be kept up by another lever, which had an effect that corresponded to putting on the loud pedal in a modern piano. The keyboard lever had another lifter on it, which struck up against the undersides of the strings little hammers, hinged at one end, and hanging down underneath. Readers who are interested in music should go to South Kensington, where, if they apply at the office, they will be shown the working parts of the exhibits. It will make playing more interesting to them, when they understand how much patient and delicate work has been done to make it possible. The museum has some splendid examples of musical instruments throughout the ages. Antonio Stradivari made his best violins of the eighteenth century between 1700 and 1725; and Giuseppe Guarneri was his rival.

Figs. 150 and 151 give the music of "Under the Greenwood Tree", by Thomas Arne (1710–78), which has been chosen as a representative song of the period.

COOKERY AND KITCHENS

Fig. 153 shows the sort of fireplace that was common to farmhouse kitchens and cottages for several centuries. With plenty of width, sufficient depth was provided to make room for seats on either hand; and across the opening in front ran a sturdy oak beam, often with a little curtain underneath it. Sometimes, at the side of the seats, little cupboards were arranged, where pipes and tobacco could be kept, and a bottle of spirits on which duty had not been paid—if the exciseman were a friend, and the night cold, he asked no questions. Small recesses in the brickwork enclosed a stock of tinder and matches. Tinder was made by putting woollen or cotton rags into the fire, then, once they were alight, placing them in the bottom of the tinder-box and covering them with the damper, which was a sheet of metal

152 A Kitchen Crane, from a Farmhouse at Biggin Hill, Kent

fitting down into the box. The steel was a piece of metal bent round and held in the left hand, and struck with a piece of flint until a spark dropped on to the tinder. The spark was blown up and the match lighted from the glow. The match was a thin strip of wood dipped into brimstone. Lucifer matches were not introduced until well on in the nineteenth century.

The wood fire itself seldom went out from one year's end to the other; and when the farmer came down very early in the

153 A Cottage Interior with an old Woman getting her Tea
From a Painting by W. B. Bigg, R.A., 1783, in the Victoria and Albert Museum

154 An Iron Foundry, *c.* 1780
From an Engraving after J. Wright of Derby

morning he raked the ashes until he found some still glowing, and then put on dry faggots and blew up the fire with the bellows. The ashes were not cleared away, because they gave the heart to the fire. The outer edges were capital places to cook potatoes in, or broil in their skins mushrooms turned cup uppermost. Saucepans had small iron trivets, or stands, so that they could be pushed into the hot ashes. Pots were suspended over the fire from wrought-iron cranes, as illustrated in fig. 152. This example is from Kent, and shows how the crane can be swung horizontally, and the pot moved up and down, by the lever that fits into the projecting knobs on the strip at the back. They were practical fellows, the old smiths! In cottages a simpler ratchet arrangement was used. An iron rod, suspended from a bar in the chimney, had a loose clip at the bottom end. This clip fitted over the saw-like teeth of a flat piece of metal, which at its upper end was arranged to work up and down on the iron rod by a ring; at its lower end was the hook for the pot, the height of which could be adjusted by the clip and the ratchet. We illustrate this type with "idle-back" attachment in Vol. III. All the interior fittings of the cottage illustrated in fig. 153 are worthy of close examination.

The fire-dogs, for holding up the wood, had hooks on the front, in which were placed the long spits, reaching across the front of the fire from dog to dog. The joint or fowl to be roasted was trussed on to the spit, which, if a bird were being roasted, went right through the carcass. If it were a large joint, a cradle-spit was used. In this form, the main spit was divided into an oblong frame in the centre, at the ends of which were spindles with screw-threads worked on to them. This enabled two oblong hoops, with an eyelet hole at each end, to be placed over the spindles, and turned with a thumb-screw down on to the joint, which was thus securely held; or the spit had a forked prong which moved on it, and after being stuck into the joint could be screwed up tight. The spits had a pulley wheel at one end, from which lines were taken, like belting in a factory, to some such mechanical arrangement as was shown in fig. 93, or they were worked by a smoke-jack in the chimney. This consisted of a vane, turned by the upward current of hot air and smoke. In Vol. III is seen a turnspit from a Welsh inn kitchen, worked by a dog. Fire-dogs are also called andirons, brandirons and brand-dogs; sometimes the tops of the standard were made cup-shaped, so that spiced ale might be kept warm.

When the spits were not in use, they were kept on a spit rack over the mantelshelf outside. The latter came just above the beam across the opening, and held the "Toby" jugs, brass candlesticks, and other treasures of the housewife.

An iron fire-back rose behind the fire, often very beautifully decorated with heraldic emblems. The bacon was placed in a smoke-chamber, formed in the flue over the fire, and so arranged that the bacon could be put in from a staircase, or upper floor, at the side of the chimney. Gilbert White writes to his friend Pennant in 1771: "There is a small, long, shining fly in these parts, very troublesome to the housewife, by getting into the chimneys, and laying its eggs in the bacon while it is drying."

The toasting-dog depicted in fig. 155 is made of wood—a gay little fellow, about the same size as a fox-terrier. Please note how obligingly his tail has been turned into a handle.

Gilbert White's *Natural History of Selborne* grew out of a series of letters that, beginning in 1767, he addressed to two of his friends—Thomas Pennant, a Welsh naturalist, and Daines Barrington, who was interested in the same subject. These letters were not at first intended for publication; but they proved so interesting that White's correspondents suggested that they should be brought out in book form; which was done in 1789. Apart from their scientific value, White's letters appeal to us, as does *Pepys's Diary*, because the author possessed a highly developed gift of observation. Little did Gilbert White, Fellow of Oriel, think, as he sat in his garden at Selborne, watching the birds and afterwards describing what he had noted for his friends' benefit, that he was laying the foundations of a famous book! He must have been a charming old man, and perhaps Austin

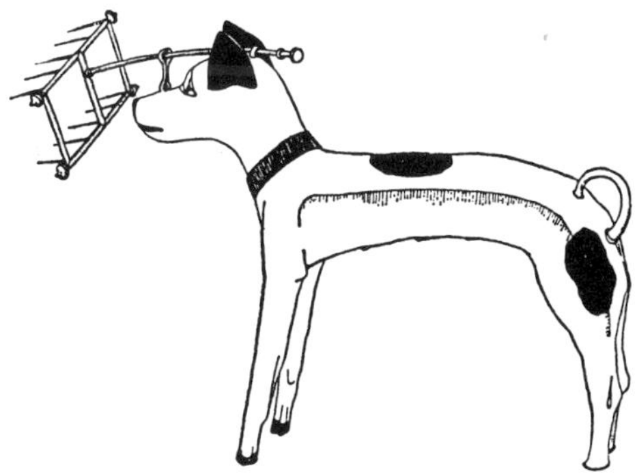

155 A Toasting-Dog from a House in Suffolk

Dobson had him in mind when he wrote of an eighteenth-century country gentleman:

He lived in that past Georgian day,
When men were less inclined to say
That "Time is Gold", and overlay
  With toil their pleasure;
He held some land, and dwelt thereon,
Where, I forget,—the house is gone;
His Christian name, I think, was John,
  His surname, Leisure.

One of White's letters to Barrington, written on November 1st, 1775, is about "the use of rushes instead of candles". We are told that the common soft rush was used and gathered in the summer and autumn.

> As soon as they are cut they must be flung into water, and kept there; for otherwise they will dry and shrink, and the peel will not run. At first a person would find it no easy matter to divest a rush of its peel, or rind, so as to leave one regular, narrow, even rib from top to bottom that may support the pith. . . . When these *junci* are thus prepared, they must lie out on the grass to be bleached and take the dew for some nights, and afterwards be dried in the sun. Some address is required in dipping these rushes in scalding fat, or grease. . . . The careful wife of an industrious Hampshire labourer obtains all her fat for nothing; for she saves the scummings of her bacon-pot for this use: and if the grease abounds with salt, she causes the salt to precipitate to the bottom, by setting the scummings in a warm oven.

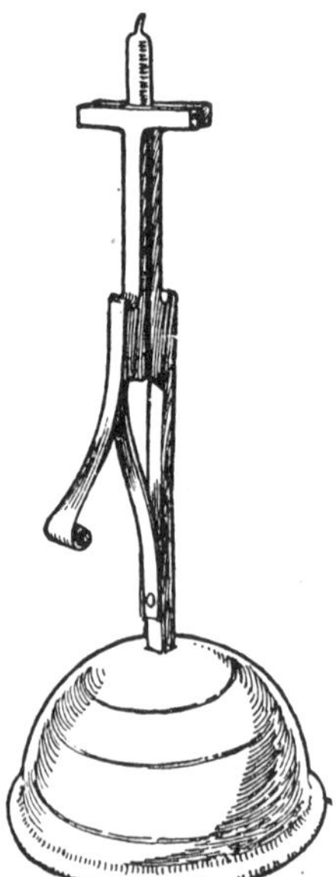

156 A Rush-light Holder

We are told that a good rush, 2 feet 4½ inches long,

> burnt only three minutes short of an hour, and gave a good clear light; watch-lights (coated with tallow), it is true, shed a dismal one; but then, the wicks of these have two ribs of the rind, or peel, to support the pith,

while the wick of the dipped rush has but one. The two ribs are intended to impede the progress of the flame, and make the candle last.

White gives some interesting calculations. 1,600 rushes weigh 1 lb. Assuming each rush burnt for only half an hour, a poor man obtained 800 hours' light for 3*s*. This was based on 1 lb. of rushes using up 6 lb. of grease in dipping; and, if the rushes were bought, they cost 1*s*. per lb. and the grease 4*d*. per lb. A working-class family used about 1½ lb. of rushes, or 2,400 lights, in the year. "Little farmers," says White, "use rushes much in the short days, both morning and evening, in the dairy and kitchen." Fig. 156 shows the rush-light holder in which they were used.

There is an interesting note in White's *Natural History* which shows that metheglin, a fermented liquor made from honey, was being made in 1775: "When metheglin was making, he would linger round the tubs and vessels, begging a draught of what he called bee-wine."

GARDENS AND GARDEN BUILDINGS

Fig. 157 shows a garden house at the end of George I's reign—an amusing little hexagonal structure. Our readers must be used to plans; so we need not explain the meaning of the small diagram shown at the lower left-hand corner. It has been taken at the level of the seats, and illustrates how cleverly they have been arranged. The right-hand plan shows the circular dome imposed on the hexagonal cornice. Any reader who enjoys designing might try the effect of an octagonal treatment. It is great fun experimenting with geometrical figures; and those who are architecturally minded should study the steeples of Wren's City churches, and see how he worked up from perhaps a square base, through all sorts of shapes, to a circular dome. It is these large shapes, and the structure of the building, that settle its architectural character and success, rather than the mouldings and carving, which are only trimmings.

A pleasant feature of this garden house is the plaster vault, springing out from over the seats to just behind the architrave of the entablature. The columns under the latter are of the Doric order. On the frieze of the entablature are shown small projections with vertical sinkings; these are called triglyphs, the

157 A Garden House, end of George I's Reign
Founded on a Temple in the Garden of The Moot, Downton, Wiltshire

space between is the metope, and in ancient classical buildings these spaces were often decorated with ox-skulls carved in relief.

GARDENS AND GARDEN BUILDINGS

Gardens until about this time continued to be designed in the formal manner described on page 76. There were fine avenues of trees, fish-ponds and bowling-greens, clipped yew hedges and topiary work, terraces and flights of steps, enlivened with beautiful stone and lead vases and garden sculpture. Then a sad change came about in the middle and end of the century, as a reaction against the formalism of the older gardens, which people began to find dull. Addison wrote in *The Spectator* that he disliked "trees rising in cones, globes, and pyramids", and that "he would rather look upon a tree in all its luxuriancy and diffusion of boughs and branches". William Kent, the architect, laid out gardens, and as he worked on the principle of "Nature abhors a straight line", obviously the old formal gardens did not appeal to him. He tried to make his gardens as natural in appearance as he could, and even went to the length of planting occasional dead trees "to give the greater air of truth to the scene"!

Lancelot Brown, born in 1715, was a pupil of Kent, and followed the same principles. He was nicknamed "Capability" Brown, because he was fond of talking of the capabilities of any garden or park that he was called in to "improve" and destroy, and this he did in so ruthless a fashion that comparatively few gardens of an earlier period remain to show us what they were like. He destroyed the gardens at Buckingham House, described on page 210; but he was a very successful and much-consulted man, becoming the Royal Gardener at Hampton Court, where he planted the celebrated vine in 1769.

Sir William Chambers, another architect, published a book on *Oriental Gardening* in 1772, and designed the pagoda at Kew in the fashionable Chinese manner. His work in this style was always restrained and kept within limits. Other men, without his knowledge, produced some amazing freaks; but the miniature Temple of Æolus at Kew, also designed by Chambers, not in the Chinese, is a more interesting piece of work.

Chambers hoped to infuse a greater degree of imagination into the design of English gardens.

> Our gardens [he complained in his book] differ very little from common fields, so closely is common nature copied in most of them. There is generally so little variety in the objects, such a poverty of imagination in the contrivance, and of art in the

arrangement, that these compositions rather appear the offspring of chance than design, and a stranger is often at a loss to know whether he is walking in a meadow or in a pleasure-ground, made and kept at a considerable expense.

COACHES, CARRIAGES, AND WAGONS

Country houses and gardens suggest the coaches that brought their owners down from London; and, as the years go by, we find that Englishmen become more and more devoted to travelling. Fashionable persons went to stay at Tunbridge Wells, Epsom, Bath, and Cheltenham. Sea-bathing became popular, and there is a print of Scarborough sands in 1735, showing quite a substantial bathing-machine, and people swimming in the sea. Later, Margate, Brighton, and Weymouth also arose as fashionable watering-places.

The subject of travel is always an absorbing one. First, saddle-horses seem to have been most generally used; for, like the pack-horses employed to carry merchandise, they could pick their way over rough and narrow roads. Parties of people on foot often accompanied the pack-horses, taking advantage of the safety afforded by numbers. At the end of the sixteenth century, large broad-wheeled wagons travelled between towns with goods and passengers, and were called stages. Hackney coaches began to appear about 1605, and stage-coaches about 1640, the latter being like large private coaches. Outside passengers sat in a basket between the hind wheels, or sat on the roof, as shown by Hogarth in a picture painted in 1730. Mail coaches were started towards the end of the eighteenth century; and letters before this were delivered by the post-boys, who took the private coaches by stages. Gloucester was a day's journey from London, and Hereford 1½ days. There were amusing disputes in the eighteenth century about road-making. Laws were passed stipulating that the stage-wagons should have very wide wheels, to assist in rolling the roads; but to this the proprietors of the wagons strongly objected. Roads were built and maintained by the parishes, who levied tolls from those who travelled on them.

> Carriages should always be built adapted to the places for which they are destined [wrote Mr. Felton, an eighteenth-century coach-builder, in the year 1790], whether for town, country, or the

> Continent; as a greater stress is laid upon the carriages in drawing over stones than on a smooth road. This makes it absolutely necessary to build stronger for the town than if intended for the country only, owing to the general goodness of our English roads; it is also necessary to build stronger for the Continent than even for the town, as the badness of their roads obliges them to use six horses where we should use two.

This means that the roads in towns were paved with granite cobbles, which would badly shake the framework of a carriage. In the seventeenth and early eighteenth centuries there were no pavements; but foot passengers were protected by lines of posts along the side walks, as can be seen in the views of Hogarth and Loggan. Later in the eighteenth century, pavements, as we have them now, came into use.

Fig. 158 shows a post-chaise, or a chaise in which one posted from town to town, hiring the horses at the posting-houses. It has a straight perch, rather like the timber wagon in fig. 94; but the place of the standards has now been taken by upright springs, from the ends of which the chariot-shaped body is suspended by leather braces, with additional straps over to keep it steady. Luggage was carried on the front transom and back axle-tree, and on the roof as well.

Fig. 159 is of a perch phaeton of 1790—the sporting conveyance of the time; the fact that it was undoubtedly dangerous probably added a zest to its use. There are double perches of a graceful swan-neck pattern. The body is attached to upright springs in

158 A Post-Chaise

159 A Perch Phaeton, 1790

front, and suspended by leather braces from others at the back, with additional straps to prevent swaying. Luggage was carried fore and aft.

Fig. 160 shows a gig; and again the body is suspended from curved springs by leather braces. When the body was fixed in the shafts, with long horizontal springs beneath attached to the axle-trees, it became a whisky. A one-horse phaeton was like a gig on four wheels; a curricle, a gig drawn by two horses; a cabriolet, a gig with a hood.

Landaus was first made in 1757, at the German town of that name. As in a coach, the upper part was made to open in halves, and fall back at an angle. Landaulets were chariots made to open. Sulkies contained only one person, and by the French were called *Anglaises désobligeantes*.

Fig. 161 shows an old wagon from Kent, the main interest of which is in the shape of the body. Nowadays the wagon is rather like a square box, the front wheels being small enough to turn round under the body. But small wheels are bad for drawing over farmland, because the smaller bearing surface cuts in; so in the older types, used for farmwork and soft roads, the front wheels were kept larger, and this necessitated the body having a waist into which the wheels could go on turning. This waist, with the curved lines of the top, gave the old wagons a look of the ship; and, as they bumped across the stubbles, it did not need a great deal of imagination to think of them as galleons,

160 A Gig

pitching and dipping and curtseying to the sea. It would be pleasant to go back to the days when we played in wagons and pretended they were ships. Like the galleon, the wagon was gaily painted.

Fig. 162 gives some details of an old wagon, and examples of the work done with the draw-shave. This was a knife-shaped tool, about 12 inches long, with a handle at each end; and, as it was drawn towards you, a shaving peeled off. Though the main object of its use was to reduce the weight of the wagon and save the horses, at the same time it afforded the wheelwright an opportunity to ornament his work.

161 An Old Wagon

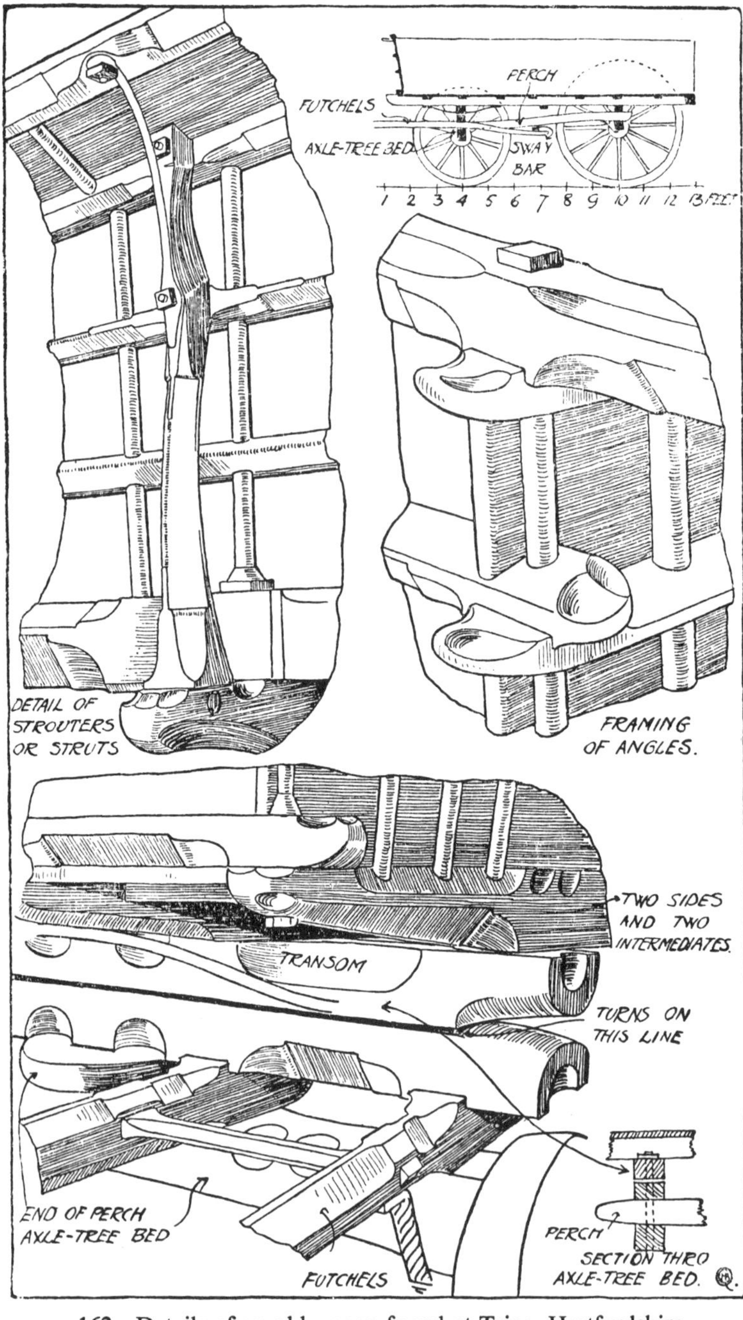

162 Details of an old wagon found at Tring, Hertfordshire

The village wheelwright was the great country craftsman. He made the wagons and carts, the ploughs and harrows. Some such man must have been responsible for the wooden hay rake(163) which we discovered on a farm in Norfolk. It is 11 feet 9 inches long, and made on the same principle as a comb. It was pulled by a horse; and, when sufficient hay or corn had been collected, the horse was stopped and backed, and the rake pulled back by the small iron handle at the side of the wooden one. This latter was then pushed down; so that the rake rode over the collected hay when the horse was restarted.

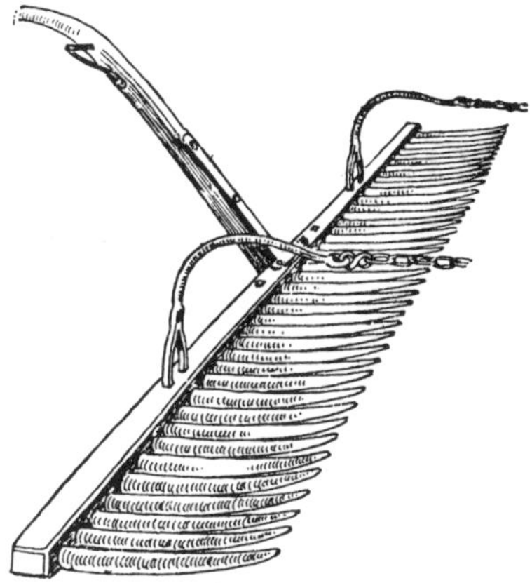

163 A Wooden Hay Rake from a Farm in Norfolk

All should read *The Wheelwright's Shop*, by George Sturt, a delightful book by a working wheelwright, published in 1923. A sister volume on *The Village Carpenter* was issued in 1937 by Walter Rose of Haddenham, Buckinghamshire.

CLUBS AND PLACES OF AMUSEMENT

As men became more travelled, they felt the need of common meeting-places, where they could see their friends and discuss the news of the day. We have mentioned the "Mermaid Tavern", where Shakespeare and Jonson indulged in combats of wit. Pepys was a sociable sort of person, and liked to go to the coffee-houses, where, as he said, there was much "admirable discourse", and the custom was continued by Londoners of the eighteenth century. Boswell's *Life of Johnson* contains many accounts of such meetings; and, though the Doctor was rather fond of putting Boswell in his place, most of the evenings they passed together appear to have been very happy occasions. Eighteenth-century London was, of course, a much smaller and less densely populated place than it is today, and the circle of an educated man's acquaintance would seem to have been larger and more friendly. It was during this period that the club developed out of the coffee-house, to meet the demand for a more aristocratic and exclusive meeting-place, where men of the same social standing could come together. These clubs were often run by individuals for their own profit, with a committee of members. Almack's was founded in 1764, and became Brooks's in 1778. Unlimited gambling took place there, and many notable men were members. Among others may be mentioned Charles James Fox, Pitt, Burke, Sir Joshua Reynolds, Garrick, Walpole, and Sheridan. Fig. 164 shows the gaming room in an eighteenth-century club. Horace Walpole thus describes a gathering of gamesters:

> They began by pulling off their embroidered clothes and put on frieze greatcoats, or turned their coats inside outwards for luck. They put on pieces of leather such as are worn by footmen when they clean knives to save their lace ruffles; and to guard their eyes from the light and to prevent tumbling their hair, they wore high-crowned hats with broad brims, and adorned with flowers and

164 A Gaming Room
Brooks's Club, London

ribbons and masks to conceal their emotions, and each gamester had a small neat stand by him to hold a wooden bowl with an edge of ormolu to hold his rouleaux.

The great gambling period in England extended from the reign of Queen Anne to that of Victoria, and reached its height at the end of the eighteenth century—perhaps because the constant wars and the change-over to industrialism had unsettled men's minds and inspired them with a mood of restlessness and recklessness. Hazard was the principal game played. Faro started in 1780, an adaptation of the Stuart game of basset. Whist, curiously enough, started in servants' halls, and at first bore the undignified name of "Swobbers".

THE CIRCUS

These notable men of the eighteenth century, winning and losing fortunes while Europe was in the state of ferment that led up to the French Revolution, do not present a pleasant spectacle; so we turn with pleasure to more innocent amusements. Fig. 165 is of a circus—a form of amusement that, luckily, is still with us, though nowadays not quite so popular as it was a hundred years ago. At its best, the old-fashioned circus provided an entrancing spectacle. Horses thundered around the ring, and beautiful ladies jumped through paper-covered hoops. The ringmaster, a superb if somewhat haughty individual, was in charge of the proceedings, and the clown won all our young admiration by his sallies. Over all this part of the performance was cast a lovely scent compounded of oranges and tan, horses and elephants, which seemed like incense offered up to pleasure. Then followed the pantomime, which was a real one, with a transformation scene, worthy, we thought, of Inigo Jones; and last came the harlequinade. Our old friend the clown reappeared with Harlequin and Columbine, who was always very lovely. Someone stole some sausages; a policeman appeared; and the show culminated in a general frolic. To understand how the romantic traditions of the circus are still kept alive, the reader should turn to J. S. Clarke's *Circus Parade*, published in 1936, with many fine pictures.

The travelling circus is still with us, and occasionally displays are given in large buildings; but such performances lack the traditional character of those given in a permanent circus. The

165 A Circus

circus illustrated bears some resemblance to the Elizabethan theatre(52); and the latter, as we saw, developed out of the bear-pit. Probably all theatres could be traced back to the ancient arenas, where displays of horsemanship and gladiatorial combats were exhibited.

The circus became popular during the second half of the eighteenth century. In the *Microcosm of London*, we are told that in the early days of George III's reign

> a man excited the curiosity and called forth the wonder of the metropolis, by riding a single horse, on full gallop, while standing upright on the saddle. This person first exhibited in a field near Bancroft's almshouses, at Mile End; the place was enclosed with boards, to prevent any gratuitous view of the exercise, and the price of the admittance was one shilling.

This individual was so successful that he retired, and set himself up in the principal inn in Derby on his savings.

Philip Astley started giving equestrian performances on a piece of ground in the Westminster Bridge Road in 1774; and here again the display was given in the open, behind boarded fences. Then the space was roughly covered in; and, later, a more permanent building which had been erected was burned down. At the beginning of the nineteenth century, Philip's son built the one shown in our illustration, which was called Astley's Royal Amphitheatre. In the morning the circus was used as a riding-school; and it must be remembered that at this time everybody had to learn to ride.

As to the performances to be seen in the eighteenth-century circus, we do not think we can do better than to give an extract from an advertisement of 1780:

> Part I will consist of the Lilliputian World, or Chinese Shadows: . . . Scene I—A curious Opera Dancer, with all the new Attitudes, in a comic Dance called the Dutch Woman. Scene II—The Dock Yard, with a Representation of the several Artists at work on a large Ship, to conclude with a Song on Admiral Rodney's Victory over the Spaniards, by Mr. Connel. Scene III—The Lion Catchers [unfortunately no details are given of this]. Scene IV—The Broken Ridge, with a Song by Mr. Wilkinson. Scene V—The Duck Hunters. Scene VI—The Storm, etc. The whole of the above Exhibition to conclude with a Hornpipe, in a most extraordinary manner. Between the Acts of the Chinese Shadows will be presented an exhibition called the Theatre of Florence, representing several frontispieces of beautiful Fireworks, which have been displayed in different parts of Europe.

Then followed—

> Horsemanship on a Single Horse—Tumbling and other agility of body—Horsemanship on two and three horses, in a manner truly entertaining—Slack Rope Vaulting on full swing in different attitudes—Polanders' tricks on Chairs, Ladders, etc.—The Clown on Horseback, with several parts of Horsemanship burlesqued—The Taylor riding on the Dancer, the Hunter, and Road Horse. The whole to conclude with the amazing performance of Men piled on Men, or the Egyptian Pyramids.

THEATRES, SHOWS, AND PLEASURE-GARDENS

A grand marionette theatre was opened in St. James's Street by the poet Colley Cibber; and Smollett describes it as "the modish diversion of the time".

At Exeter Exchange, in the Strand, was a wild beast show,

containing elephants, giraffes, lions, and tigers; and doubtless children were taken to see them, and enjoyed themselves, even as children do at the Zoo today. The eighteenth century was truly a great age for amusements of all kinds; and one very noticeable feature of the day was the number of spas, or tea-gardens, that sprang up. Their forerunner was the Spring Gardens at Whitehall, where Charles I played bowls and indulged in mild entertainments. Then came the Mulberry Gardens, spoken of by Pepys, where Dryden might be seen eating tarts. It was closed in 1674. Islington Spa came into being in the early eighteenth century, being noted for its medicinal waters; the Princesses Caroline and Amelia regularly took the waters there. Bagnigge Wells acquired renown for its many kinds of alfresco entertainments, as did Marylebone Gardens, where fine singing was the chief attraction.

All these places in the early part of the century were simple and refined; and citizens of London could go there, take tea, listen to the music, and watch the varied flow of people promenading to and fro. In 1734 Peerless Pool (originally called Perilous Pool, and used for duck-hunting), situated where Old Street now runs, was turned into an open-air swimming-bath. A canal was cut from it and stocked with fish, where visitors could fish for a small fee.

As time went on, the rivalry between the different gardens caused them to vie with one another in the luxuriousness and extravagance of their entertainments. "Jenny's Whim", in Chelsea, had a bowling-green, a cockpit, and a pond where mechanical mermaids and fishes rose at intervals. There was a grotto where Harlequin and Mother Shipton started up when the visitor trod on a concealed spring. Unfortunately, the character of these places gradually declined until they became a source of public scandal, and they were suppressed by law and finally disappeared.

In fashionable London, from the reign of Queen Anne to that of George III, masked balls and assemblies were the rage. These parties were first organised as regular and public entertainments in 1708, by a Swiss named Heidegger, who was called by Henry Fielding "surintendant des plaisirs d'Angleterre". They were scenes of extraordinary brilliance; and it was no uncommon thing for a dandy to change his costume three times during the course of the same evening. The "Pantheon" in Oxford Street, Cornely's at Carlisle House and Almack's were the favourite places for such assemblies. In fact, a class of people arose who made their living—and often made a fortune—by taking a large house and organising masked assemblies there, charging so much for each ticket of entrance.

The young dandies of Almack's, White's, and Boodle's (all exclusive gaming-clubs) gave private masquerades at Carlisle House; and on one occasion 800 people were present, all in fancy dress, one lady, as an Indian sultana, having diamonds worth £100,000 on her head-dress. But the popularity of this form of amusement, like that of the tea-garden, slowly waned; many of the assemblies grew disreputable, and they were gradually given up.

CHILDREN'S BOOKS AND GAMES

Children's picture-books, sold at popular prices, first came into existence in the eighteenth century. They were mostly little chap-books, illustrated with small woodcuts, sometimes gaily coloured, generally of the favourite nursery stories—*Babes in the Wood*, *Mother Bunch*, *Dick Whittington*, *Cinderella*, *Red Riding Hood*, *The Sleeping Beauty*, *Bluebeard*, *Puss-in-Boots*, and *Little Tom Thumb*; all old tales, some so old that their origin is lost in the mists of time.

The two pictorial alphabets—*A was an Archer who shot at a frog*, and *A was an Apple-pie*—were well known in the reign of Queen Anne. These books were usually sold by travelling pedlars called chapmen, or paultrie pedlars.

For the more restless spirits there were many games—battledore and shuttlecock, marbles, hot cockles, hunt the slipper, thread the needle, trap-ball(166), and games with toy parachutes(167) and peg-tops. Football is, of course, a very old game. It is spoken of in the fifteenth century; and in the reign of James I a rule was made to "debarre from this court all rough and violent exercise as the football, meeter for laming than for making able the users

166 Trap-ball

167 A Boy with Parachute

thereof". But boys still played the game, despite the law that kings and parliaments laid down; and in Chester, Dorking, and elsewhere it was always played in the streets on Shrove Tuesday.

In an eighteenth-century print, apprentices are to be seen playing football in the Strand. Bear-leader was a favourite game(168). It was played by several children, one blind-folded, who led another on his hands and knees by a cord. The blind-folded boy was the bear-leader; and it was his duty to prevent the others hitting the bear, who crouched beside him for protection. Little girls had a game called Queen Anne, which was played thus—the children stood in two lines which faced one another, one line hiding among themselves a ball. Both lines moved backwards and forwards reciting alternate lines of the following verses:

Lady Queen Anne who sits in her stand [sedan-chair]
And a pair of green gloves upon her hand,
As white as a lily, as fair as a swan,
The fairest lady in a' the land.

Come smell my lily, come smell my rose,
Which of my maidens do you choose?
I choose you one, and I choose you all,
And I pray Miss (----) yield up the ball.

The ball is mine and none of yours,
Go to the woods and gather flowers;
Cats and kittens bide within,
But all young ladies walk out and in.

The child named Queen Anne had the task of deciding which child on the opposing side had the ball; and, if she guessed right, the ball was given up to her with a curtsey.

Until this time there were no professional manufacturers of the better-class toys; but each small object was a miniature

168 The Game of Bear-leader

replica of the full-size thing, made by the regular craftsman to whom that particular trade belonged.

For instance, very charming little complete tea and dinner services were made by the great china-makers of the day; and wonderful doll's furniture was produced by Sheraton and Chippendale themselves. Miniature kitchen sets could be obtained; and for the children of the rich silversmiths made perfect models, in silver, of almost all the everyday things one can think of. Eighteenth-century dolls' houses are charming little Georgian houses, in miniature, true to style, and not, as now, without any sense of design at all.

Lead soldiers were cast, chiefly flat, and sometimes soldiers folded and painted on paper were sold, from $5\frac{1}{2}$ to 7 inches high. Rocking-horses could be bought—in fact, most of the toys that the child of today loves were already beloved in the eighteenth century. Cheap mechanical toys, however, were not made until the end of the century, although we hear of peep-shows with dancing and musical figures. One wonderful mechanical and musical figure, 15 feet 6 inches high, called "The Flute Player", was made by a craftsman named Vancouson, and exhibited in Paris.

LEARNING, LITERATURE, AND SOCIAL HABITS

Let us now turn to another side of the picture, and see what attention was given to literature and scholarly learning.

Booksellers' shops were still comparatively rare; and in Boswell's *Life of Johnson* we read that, even in Birmingham, only one was opened—and that on market days, by Johnson's father, Michael Johnson. But many great essayists and poets were emerging; and in 1761 we hear that Sheridan delivered lectures on the English language in Edinburgh and at Bath. The first regular periodicals were published early in the eighteenth century. *The Tatler* commenced in 1709, followed by *The Spectator* in 1711, *The Guardian* and *The Rambler* in 1713, and *The Gentleman's Magazine* in 1731.

The first daily paper began to appear regularly in 1702. It measured 14 by 8 inches. Some of these newspapers were arranged with one blank sheet, in order that Londoners could buy the paper, read it, and pass it on together with a note written by themselves on the blank sheet, to their friends in the country. All the best papers could be read at the coffee-houses for the fee of a penny.

In 1730 the original Methodists came into existence; and this name was first given to a society of students at Oxford, noted for their earnest and methodical attention to devout exercises.

Certain charitable organisations were founded; and in 1789 Hannah More and her sister Patty, with the financial assistance of Wilberforce, started the Cheddar Mission. She was then about forty-six years old and spent most of her summers in a cottage she owned in a small village near Bristol. The district round the Cheddar Gorge was notorious for the savagery of its inhabitants, many of whom lived in the limestone caves in a completely wild and uncivilised state, all respectable country people giving the place a wide berth. Despite great opposition, Hannah More succeeded in establishing schools and clubs, thus helping and reclaiming and civilising hundreds of women and children.

Another society of a very different kind, called in derision the "Blue Stockings", was formed by Mrs. Elizabeth Montague and her friends, women who met for conversation only, without the usual adjunct of cards and frivolous gossip. Certain clever men also came to Mrs. Montague's *salon*; and Horace Walpole, Dr. Johnson, and Edmund Burke were frequent visitors, as, among members of the opposite sex, were Hannah More, Mrs. Thrale, and Frances Burney. Benjamin Stillingfleet, one of the shining lights in the society's discussions, was nevertheless eccentric in his dress; and it was the blue worsted stockings he affected that earned the "Bas Bleu Ladies" their nickname.

The manners of the eighteenth century were a curious mixture of coarseness and artificial elegance. Men might bow and posture and turn a compliment gracefully; yet they often used the most horrible oaths and were accustomed to enjoy the coarsest of pleasures. Great ladies too, although they were apt to swoon and languish, would also swear and spit, and beat their maids. Table manners we should find somewhat coarse today. Swift mentions the appearance of "Doiley" napkins, so named from a leading linen-draper who produced them; and in a book on table manners, published in 1703, the reader is counselled to wipe his knife on his napkin and not on his bread or on the table-cloth. Two-pronged forks were used; those with three prongs were still rare and expensive. As regards spoons, the manual of etiquette mentioned above refers to a basin being placed on the sideboard to wash them in; for "some [people] are so curious that they will not endure a spoon to be used in two several dishes". These books, however, were probably aimed at people who, having made money, wished to acquire gentility. Three o'clock was the usual dinner hour, and fashionable persons drank chocolate in their rooms in the morning. In the afternoon, the fashionable world rode, drove, or walked round Hyde Park; and in the reign of Queen Anne rules were issued as to the keeping the park in proper order. Lanterns were lit at nightfall on the road from Hyde Park to the Palace at Kensington; and we learn that at this time lamps with thick convex glass began to be used in the streets of London which gave better light by far than the former lanterns.

Even so the roads, not only in the country, but around, and indeed in, London, were unsafe at night. Bands of fashionable dissolute young men, calling themselves Mohocks, roamed the streets at night assaulting passers-by. Then came others called Scowerers, who broke up inns and disturbed meetings, always to the accompaniment of noise and brutality. Others, again, called Nickers, broke windows after dark by flicking pennies at them. Even in 1791 highway robberies were committed almost with impunity on all the roads leading out of London. Some of these roads were so unsafe that bands of armed horsemen were hired to ride with and protect coaches travelling. Piccadilly is spoken of as being "quite unsafe after dark"; and in 1748 the French mail was robbed by highwaymen as it drove along Pall Mall at half past eight in the evening.

It was not until 1805 that the Bow Street horse patrol was established by Sir Richard Ford. This consisted of thirteen parties of armed horsemen, who patrolled the roads within a 10-mile radius of London, and gradually swept them clear of highwaymen and other "evilly disposed persons"; and in 1829 Sir Robert Peel established policemen in London itself.

Shops were fewer then than they are now; and many goods were sold on barrows on the streets. Every trade had its own particular call, generally a sing-song chant. Thread laces were called, also strawberries and all fruits, gingerbread toys and alphabets, eels, and chickens, and a host of other things, many to be seen in that charming series, *Tempest's Cryes of London*. One feature of London life, that we have not yet mentioned, made its appearance in 1761.

> The artists [we read in Boswell's *Life of Johnson*] have instituted a yearly exhibition of pictures and statues, in imitation, I am told, of foreign academies. This year was the second exhibition. They please themselves much with the multitude of spectators, and imagine that the English school will rise in reputation. Reynolds is without a rival.

169 A Butcher's Shop
After Thomas Rowlandson, 1790

170 Stalls in the Old Stocks Market, 1738, on the site of the Mansion House

Engraved by H. Fletcher from a drawing by Jos. Nichols

This exhibition is of interest. Arranged by the Society of Artists, it was held in the Adelphi; and here Gainsborough first exhibited his work in London. Out of this was developed the Royal Academy of Arts, founded in 1768. Sir Joshua Reynolds was the first president, and Chambers the architect, treasurer. Bartolozzi, Cosway, Angelica Kauffmann, and Benjamin West, were among the original members; and, though Gainsborough does not figure in the list, his name is given as an R.A. in the first catalogue. Romney never became a member.

Reynolds once referred to Gainsborough as "our best landscape painter"; but curiously enough the eighteenth-century public did not buy his landscapes; and he was esteemed, like his rivals Reynolds and Romney, for his portraits. Gainsborough quarrelled with his fellow Academicians; but, when he was dying in 1788, sent for Reynolds, and almost his last words were addressed to him: "We are all going to heaven, and Vandyck is of the party." London's National Gallery enshrines many splendid examples of eighteenth-century English painting.

EIGHTEENTH-CENTURY ORNAMENT

Our tail-piece shows a typical piece of ornament, designed by Robert Adam, and as it happens also to be the end-piece, we will doff our caps, wave brush and pen, and bid our readers "Good-bye".

171 Eighteenth-century Ornament

INDEX

The numerals in **heavy type** *refer to the figure numbers of the illustrations*

INDEX